# flight

# risk

## The high and lows of life as a doctor at Heathrow Airport

DR STEPHANIE GREEN

HEADLINE

The right of Stephanie Green to be identified as the Author of the Work has been asserted by
her in accordance with the Copyright, Designs and Patents Act 1988.

First published in 2018 by
HEADLINE PUBLISHING GROUP

First published in paperback in 2019 by
HEADLINE PUBLISHING GROUP

1

Cataloguing in Publication Data is available from the British Library

ISBN 978 1 4722 5694 2

Typeset in Garamond by CC Book Production
Printed and bound in Great Britain by Clays Ltd, Elcograf S.p.A.

Headline's policy is to use papers that are natural, renewable
and recyclable products and made from wood grown in sustainable forests.
The logging and manufacturing processes are expected to conform
to the environmental regulations of the country of origin.

This is a work of non-fiction based on the author's experiences,
but the details of certain people, events, locations and dates have been altered,
and some anecdotes are composites of separate events. This has been done
solely to protect the privacy of individuals.

HEADLINE PUBLISHING GROUP
An Hachette UK Company
Carmelite House
50 Victoria Embankment
London EC4 0DZ

www.headline.co.uk
www.hachette.co.uk

# contents

# prologue

'HELLO, PORT HEALTH. Dr Green here.'

'This is Control. We've had a call from Emirates flight EK355 from Singapore, due to land at 7am. Death on board.'

It was 4am when the call had come, jolting me awake. Immediately my heart was thumping a steady rhythm as I heard the man's voice, but knowing my name and where I was felt like a positive start to the conversation.

Always the same sleepy thought: who exactly *are* Control and where are they based? Even after more than a decade of working as a doctor at the Health Control Unit (HCU) at Heathrow, I never really did find out. As far as I was concerned they were centrally located and they 'knew things'. They were disembodied voices, sporadically generating work for the small band of people working in HCU: radiographers,

Health Control Officers (HCOs), Duty Officers (DOs) . . . and me.

'Any other details?' I was sitting up in bed now.

'It was something out of the ordinary; the crew were very distressed. They contacted Medi-link [the company supplying medical assistance over the phone] after a passenger collapsed and were advised to carry out CPR, which was unsuccessful.'

'*Out of the ordinary?*'

'Will you be attending the flight, Doctor?' Control were never big on small talk.

'I will, yes. Please make sure passengers and crew remain on board until we arrive. Can you also let us know which stand the flight is coming in on with as much notice as possible?'

'Will do.'

I hung up the phone and flopped back on to my pillow. I'd never get back to sleep now. I'd been on the go since 10am the previous day – sixteen hours straight, virtually non-stop – and though my body was exhausted, my mind tended to leap out of the paddock and gallop around like mad whenever I got a call like this. It was always the same: mental checklists and action plans which generally segued into second-guessing decisions I'd made earlier that day: had I missed something from that last X-ray, when I was tired? Should I have sent the elderly man with a chest infection straight to hospital? I was usually fairly certain of my decisions when I made them, but things always seemed worse in those first few waking minutes, anxiety heightened – why was that? And what the hell did out 'of the ordinary' mean? Yes, people got sick on planes and occasionally people died on them, but for the crew to be so distressed it set my mind wondering if this death had been the result of an act of violence. Or could it even have been self-inflicted?

I'd have got up straight away if I hadn't been freezing cold. Despite swaddling my body in five – yes five – of the finest hospital blankets HCU had to offer, I still felt like I was in the depths of a Siberian winter, rather than a mild March morning in London. Heathrow has its own microclimate, with refrigerated air pumped through it whatever the season, so the temperature of my modest sleeping quarters in Terminal 4 rarely reached tepid at the best of times, and the itchy green blankets held little to no heat. I shouldn't have complained. Once the final flight had landed each night, the night-duty doctor was the only person in the whole airport who was afforded the luxury of a bed – although luxury might be pushing it as far as this particular cot went. Mandy and June, the pair of HCOs who had to doze in their chairs in the rest room outside, weren't so lucky.

It's funny; despite the fact that 650 flights landed at Heathrow every day with at least one death on board a month I never really got used to it. It wasn't so much the death part that unsettled me – as a doctor you become fairly immune to that – it was everything that went with the attendance of death. Boarding a plane full of people to do my job was like performing in front of an audience with a couple of hundred troubled eyes boring into me the whole time I worked. It always made me nervous, and with good reason. I was essentially holding an entire planeload of passengers against their will, and, having just sat through a long-haul flight with a dead body, many of them weren't all that chuffed about it. In a case where there was a body on board, passengers weren't even allowed to move out of their seats until I'd confirmed the passenger was indeed dead, and not from something that could threaten the health of the other passengers or anyone else they might come in contact with after leaving the plane.

That was one of the biggest challenges for the team at Port Health, which is the umbrella title for the entire medical team working at Heathrow's HCU: protecting the public from the entry of infectious disease into the UK. My concern when somebody died on an inbound flight was to get to the bottom of the cause before I could send the passengers out into the world, and ruling out the really scary stuff was paramount: viral haemorrhagic fevers, such as Lassa fever, Marburg disease or even Ebola, which, ten years into my job at Heathrow, we'd never had a case of in the UK. And once I was on board the plane, this all had to be executed quickly and with absolute authority. Over the years, this important drill became more performance than procedure for me, and with a tightly constructed and vigorously rehearsed script, I'd plan precisely what I was going to say, and do, before I even set foot on board. I habitually ran a mental checklist of all the items I needed to have with me too, every time I did it: pocket torch, gloves, stethoscope and thermometer. If, heaven forbid, I forgot a piece of my kit and had to dash back to HCU, not only would I be holding up a planeload of very pissed-off people, but flight schedules would be thrown off course into the bargain. Time was money. And if a plane were on the stand for even five minutes longer than scheduled, it could cost the airline concerned a fortune.

'June, are you out there?'

It was forty-five minutes before the flight was due to come in and I was up, showered and dressed, but for some reason Control still hadn't called back to let us know which stand the flight was due to land on.

'I'm here, Stephanie.' June's Scottish burr rang from the chair on the other side of the door. 'What do you need?'

'Well, I need to know where the plane's coming in,' I said, as she came in, bleary-eyed.

'Nothing from Control yet, then?' she asked.

'No, I think you'll have to call and put a rocket up them,' I told her. 'We want to be waiting for the plane rather than the other way around. This sounds like something serious.'

'I'm on it,' she said. 'Soon as I've worked out how many cups of coffee it's going to take to make me feel like a proper, human person again.'

'No sleep again, June?'

'I might as well be kipping on the runway for all the sleep I get in that bloody chair,' she said. 'Do you want some coffee, Stephanie?'

'If we've time, yes please.'

Half an hour before the flight landed, Control called to confirm that the plane would be arriving at stand 18 in Terminal 3. The terminal was a ten-minute drive away, so I needed to get my act together fast. It was barely light when I headed down to my parking space and hopped into my car, but the airport was already waking up. Fuel tankers and empty baggage trucks were orbiting the airport as I drove into the tunnel under the runway that connected Terminal 4 with the Central Terminal Area where Terminals 1, 2 and 3 were. I headed for Terminal 3's HCU to pick up more staff who would accompany me on to the flight. All Heathrow doctors attended flights with these colleagues, just in case on-board surveillance had to be carried out. When a passenger had died, or was sick, from a suspected or unidentified infectious disease, we were required to collect contact details from the other passengers. Then, once tests had been carried out to determine exactly what the disease was, passengers could be contacted if further action was required.

Often there would just be one HCO attending, but on that day there were two because of the size of the plane: an Emirates Airbus A380 – double-deck, wide-body. The largest passenger airliner in the world at the time. My attending officers that morning were Sinead and Megan. Between them, they'd clocked up years working at the airport, and although they'd most certainly attended far more deaths than I had, they still looked to me, the doctor, to take charge.

'This sounds like something quite nasty, Stephanie,' Megan said, as we headed out of HC.

'So I believe,' I said. 'Buckle up, ladies.'

As the three of us headed through Terminal 3, passengers waiting in the lounges for their flight looked bemused at the sight of me striding purposefully along in my white doctor's coat, stethoscope around my neck, as if I were about to stop and give a first aid demonstration outside Pret A Manger. I don't know why I always felt so dreadfully out of place walking through the public areas of the airport, but I did, and the nearer I got to the plane, the bigger my entourage got: police, my pair of HCOs and a handful of airline staff to deal with the fall-out of what may be about to unfold. I was a white-coated pied piper, gathering momentum as we approached the stand, while wide-eyed children clutched the hands of their rubbernecking parents, curious as to what the emergency might be.

Then my least favourite part: waiting quietly on the jetty while the plane taxied slowly to its resting point. Those few empty minutes to reflect on what might be waiting for me beyond the plane doors: some serious infectious disease? Some great risk to the UK? There was never a way of knowing until I stepped on board, and whatever it turned out to be, it was mine to deal with.

'OK, here we go.'

I headed down the jetty, my new gang in tow, while the crew member operating the air bridge shouted at us to hold tight. He lined up the electric platform with the door of the plane with a joystick, and the moving walkway shifted beneath our feet like one of those fun houses at the fairground as we were manoeuvred towards the plane, jerking this way and that. When the air bridge was in place and the hood was suctioned around the plane door, the driver banged on the door to let the crew inside know he was in position. Then the door swung open, and I was greeted by the purser.

'Port Health?' She looked relieved to see me.

'Yes, Dr Green,' I said.

I glanced over her shoulder into the eyes of a tearful young stewardess, who was steadying herself on the arm of a male colleague.

# prologue

'Thank you for coming so quickly, Doctor,' the purser said. 'It's been a bit of a rough night.'

'So I can see,' I said, my gaze still fixed on the girl. 'Is she OK?'

I was used to seeing the cabin crew looking immaculate as I entered a plane, but this poor stewardess looked anything but, and had what I feared was blood down the front of her shirt. What the hell had happened on this plane?

I pulled my gaze away from the bloodstained stewardess and once again turned my attention to the purser, whose pristine make-up, hair and attire after a traumatic, overnight, long-haul flight stood in stark contrast against the pale, exhausted apparition with no make-up and her hair scraped back in a ponytail standing before her – me.

'The gentleman is lying in one of the galleys, which we've closed off,' she said.

I stepped on to the plane, with Sinead and Megan close behind me.

'Could one of you find the man's passport to get his details for our records, please?' I asked Megan.

'Yes, Stephanie.'

I whispered a tiny prayer of thanks when the purser told me that the body was in the galley closest to the front, covered with a blanket. At least I only needed to walk past the first few rows, rather than the entire length of the silent plane with 300 pairs of eyes trained squarely on me, so I wouldn't be recording death in the cabin in full view. It was always daunting, boarding a plane to confirm a death. I was acutely aware that everyone was looking to me to decide, or at the very least make an educated guess about, what the passenger had died of, and to make the call on whether or not it was safe for everyone to disembark. It was all about me, in fact, and never a responsibility I took lightly. You'd be surprised at just how many passengers get stroppy at the idea of being held back from immediately disembarking, despite the gravity of an on-board death. I'd experienced people refusing to sit down or even listen to my announcements on some flights, too eager to jump up and retrieve their belongings from the overhead lockers to care about anything else that was going on. On one flight from Pakistan, I thought the passengers looked as if they were about ready to charge the doors if I kept them much longer.

It was for this reason that I tried never to make eye contact with the passengers unless absolutely necessary. I looked straight ahead as I made my way along the aisle. I didn't want to invite questions of any sort. All I wanted was to get the job done and get off the plane. Even after ten years, I never found it easy treating a sick passenger on a flight – undoing their clothes, checking their vital signs and listening to their heart, all under the watchful eyes of everyone else on board. It's a difficult place to do work, and the antithesis of what you get used to in the privacy of a consulting room. It's medicine-on-view and it really affects your practice: quick diagnoses, quick decisions about whether I can get the patient back to the unit where I can examine them properly and in private.

I wasn't one for attending flights in full protective clothing either, as some doctors did. I imagined it would terrify the life out of everybody on board seeing me striding down the aisle in full protective get-up, so I didn't wear it unless absolutely crucial. I usually wore my white doctor's coat and gloves, and carried my torch and a thermometer – not that there was going to be much need for a thermometer on this particular occasion.

'He's in here,' the purser said, stepping aside to let me into the galley. 'We all did the best we could.'

'I'm sure you did,' I said. 'Thank you.'

I'd seen a fair few bodies in my time, but this one was a particularly shocking sight. Probably the most disturbing I'd ever seen, certainly on a plane. The entire front of the man was covered in blood. His mouth and nostrils were caked with dried blood as well. He was a slim man and obviously wasn't that old – maybe early fifties. His skin was waxy but his face was slightly red and flushed, unusual for the dead, and his t-shirt was also covered in dried blood, which had turned a familiar dusky brown. When there's a lot of blood but no wound, the blood has usually come from somewhere in the gut, and that seemed to be the case here.

It was clear that the man was dead – no one would have needed to examine him closely to determine that – but there's a particular process I had to go through before I could confirm the death. I gathered myself and listened for breath and heart sounds, and then I shone my torch into his pupils, which were fixed, dilated and non-reactive to light. No brain stem working. I recorded the death, making a note of the time and informing Sinead, and then covered the man's face with the blanket again.

Back outside the galley, the purser introduced me to the young woman who'd dealt with the situation – the tear- and blood-streaked stewardess I'd seen as I got on – whose name was Cassie.

'Cassie, I'm Dr Green, how are you doing?'

'I'm a bit calmer now but it was really horrible,' she said.

There's no privacy on a plane; nowhere to talk. Everyone's eyes were on us so we had to duck back behind the galley area to keep the details as private as possible, although I made sure Cassie was facing away from the body so she didn't have to look at him again, even covered up with a blanket.

'Can you tell me what happened?' I asked. Calm but firm. 'What were the first signs that something was wrong?'

# prologue

'He seemed fine at first, but said he didn't want any food as he was feeling sick. Just water. Then he got up and went to one of the bathrooms and was there for quite a while.'

'And what happened after that?' I said, softly.

'He came out a bit later. He was vomiting blood, all blood. Loads of it. The look on his face, so frightened. I was frightened. I rushed to help him, but he fell on the floor and seemed to lose consciousness very quickly. I did everything I could, Doctor.'

I looked down at her clothes, where she had obviously tried to clean off the the man's splattered blood. 'Of course you did.'

'I called the other crew over, but there was still more blood so we put out the call for a doctor on board, but there was no one so . . .' Cassie trailed off, breathing in and out deeply.

'You called Medi-link?'

'The purser called Medi-link, yes, and they recommended we started CPR, which we tried but it was so difficult because of all the bleeding.'

The man had begun vomiting pure, fresh blood 38,000 feet up, and never stopped. Vomiting after massive internal bleeding – haematemesis to give it its technical name – is a horrible way to die. There were two likely causes: a gastric ulcer eroding into an artery, or ruptured oesophageal varices, which are swollen veins usually caused by alcoholism that can swell

13

until they burst, causing copious bleeding. It must have been terrifying to know you are internally bleeding in an aeroplane with no help at hand. It would have been a grisly sight for the surrounding passengers too. In haematemesis, a lot of blood is lost very quickly and visibly. It's a catastrophic event and often fatal, even in the safety of a hospital, let alone the aisle of a plane in mid-flight. There's very little anyone could have done. In a hospital, the man might have been rushed into surgery for banding of the varices (where the surgeon uses an endoscope to find the bleeding veins and applies rubber bands to them), or had a special gadget with a balloon on the end inserted into his oesophagus, then inflated in an attempt to compress the vessels and stop the bleeding. It's hard enough for medical professionals to deal with that amount of blood, let alone the untrained airline crew with no equipment. Generally, people who die on flights do so quickly and with a lot less mess, so I really felt for this brave stewardess who had stayed with the man until the end.

'We carried him – well, we sort of dragged him – into the galley so he was out of sight of the other passengers,' Cassie went on. 'Thank God a lot of them were asleep by then.'

'But you were wearing gloves?' I said.

'Yes, from the medical kit.'

'And you're sure none of the blood came into direct contact with your skin or into any cuts you might have?'

'I'm pretty sure. And I've cleaned myself up as much as I can,' she said.

'OK. Make sure anything with blood on it is disposed of as hazardous waste,' I said.

Cassie nodded, still teary-eyed. 'I absolutely will.'

'There's nothing more you could have done for him,' I said, offering a smile. 'You did everything you possibly could have.'

It struck me as odd, not to mention unfortunate, that there was no doctor on board, which was hardly ever the case on flights I've attended. In fact, it's always my dread when I'm travelling somewhere by plane that I'll get called upon to assist in an emergency, mid-flight, after a couple of gin and tonics. Doctors have a duty to help if called upon, and to do whatever is within their capability at that moment. On this flight, I was simply there to rule out an infectious disease or anything suspicious and then to record his death. So as far as those two things went, my job was done. I thanked the other members of the crew for their quick thinking and diligence in a tough situation, and then headed to the front of the plane, passing on all the relevant information to the on-board staff and the two police officers, who also had to be there to attend the death. As I was about to disembark, the pilot emerged from the cockpit.

'Thanks, Doctor. Is there anything else you need?'

'I don't think so,' I said. 'There's no reason to suspect an infectious cause of death, so we won't need to get everyone's details. You can disembark the passengers now.'

It does sometimes feel a little strange, telling the pilot what can and can't happen on their plane, but technically my authority overrides theirs in these situations and they are looking to me to make a decision, so I don't have much choice.

I never learned anything personal about the man who'd died, except that he had a passport from the United Arab Emirates and that he had been travelling alone. My only concern was to try to determine the cause of his death (or at least exclude an infectious one). The authorities would handle all his personal information once they had his name and passport number. They would also handle the practicalities like contacting the UAE Embassy and forwarding his luggage.

So much of what we doctors did, even in a setting as dramatic as Heathrow, was mechanical. Our X-ray machines whirred away, verifying diseases or concealed drugs; pregnancies were confirmed with a touch of the belly; people with unidentified symptoms were quarantined. It's not the medicine that was fascinating and unique but the people on whom we practised. That's why each time I recorded a death, I always wrote 'Rest in Peace' in my notes after the name of the deceased. As a new doctor, I had learned this practice from a senior colleague who always did the same, and it just struck me as the right thing to do; a tiny bit of humanity that comes in where the medicine ends, and an acknowledgment that this was a real person with a family, friends, a home and a life.

'Rest in Peace.'

# 1

# top secret

IT WASN'T PART OF SOME GRAND PLAN to become a doctor, but then I was never one for plans, grand or otherwise. In truth, I had no idea what I wanted to do when I left school and I certainly hadn't considered medicine – at least no more than I'd considered anything else. I kicked off my university career on a degree course in natural sciences, which turned out to be a serious undertaking and far too much like hard work – Monday to Friday, nine to four, *and* Saturday mornings. I realised that this outlandish schedule would totally cramp my style in terms of drinking and partying, but in the end it was drinking and partying that won the day. In fact, I only ever made one Saturday lecture in the first year. So, in my second and third year, I swapped to biological anthropology. Now, I'd like to be able to tell you that I had a calling to specialize in the biological evolution of the human race, but in truth it was a much easier degree involving about four hours a week of lectures (apparently, Prince Charles had done it as part of his degree). Still, I had three years at Downing College, Cambridge, which was good enough for me and I made the most of it. Besides the partying I did work extremely hard while I was at university. Despite still not having a clue where I was headed career-wise, I knew that whatever it was I wanted to be good at it – the best – and to be the best I needed all the mental ammunition I could soak up.

Most of my work experience so far had been in retail, with my first full-time job working in my mother's and step-father's shop. They'd recently given up their jobs – moving from Chester where I grew up – and bought the village store in Olveston, West Gloucestershire, where I worked the summer I left Cambridge.

My parents had divorced when I was seven and my mum, Hilary, married my stepfather Ian a couple of years later, so I'd grown up with him. By the time I was ready for senior school they'd already had two more children, while I'd been accepted to an all-girls private school. This wasn't something my parents would have been able to fund themselves, but I'd achieved high marks in the entrance exam so I was lucky enough to be offered a Government Assisted Place. Still, I always had weekend and holiday jobs: babysitting, shop work or whatever was going, because I like having financial independence, and this approach carried me right through my school years to my time at Cambridge.

Back then, of course, there weren't the huge fees that often plunge students into debt for years, but like any student I had living costs. Still, I remained self-sufficient, preferring to make my own cash instead of relying on the bank of Mum and Dad. I probably wasn't the greatest shop assistant in the world, but I enjoyed the work and put my back into it, as I did into everything. I might have had a solidly middle-class upbringing, and I am so grateful for the encouragement and support both my parents gave me, but I certainly wasn't born with the proverbial silver spoon in my mouth.

Like many Cambridge students, I took the Civil Service exams in my final year; the government often invited those with the highest scores to become top-level civil servants and I quite liked the idea of working in the Foreign Office. About a week after the exam, an unmarked envelope appeared in my college pigeonhole with a letter asking if I'd be interested in what they described as an 'alternative foreign service career'. No explanation of what it might be. Nothing. All it did say was that if I were at all interested, I was to go for an interview at an address in Whitehall the following week.

At the bottom of the page lay a sinister instruction in bold capitals: PLEASE DO NOT TELL ANYONE ABOUT THIS LETTER. All very intriguing for a twenty-one-year-old with a sense of adventure so, of course, I signed up and went along.

All along Whitehall are imposing, classical white stone buildings, but I was directed to what must have been the smallest door in Christendom and greeted by a smiling, neat woman adorned in twinset and pearls – a dead ringer for Miss Moneypenny – who led me inside. The interior of the building was nothing less than palatial, with majestic artwork and chandeliers a gogo. I was both thrilled and daunted in equal measure. 'Moneypenny' then led me to a room that was anything but palatial – a couple of chairs, a table and not much else – but she said nothing. Sitting at the table was a man who offered me a seat, a cup of coffee and a copy of the Official Secrets Act to sign but no inkling of what I was there for. My mind started racing. Should I read this through? Should I just sign it? I decided that I didn't have much choice. It would be undignified to make a bolt for it, and, as nervous as I was, I was also dying to know where all this was heading. So there I was, signing the Official Secrets Act with no idea why. What could possibly go wrong?

I handed the papers to the man who then gave me a dossier on which every single page was stamped, in bold red, 'TOP SECRET'.

I peered down at it, wondering what on earth might be

expected of me. Was this someone's idea of an elaborate joke or had I stumbled on to the set of a cut-price Bond movie? I suddenly felt small in the midst of it all. Nobody had explained a single thing to me about why I was there and what the position was, all they'd said was 'sit down, sign this, read this'. I remember thinking how ludicrous it was that an important government document should have those great big red words plastered all over it if they didn't want people to bloody well read it. Surely, if one sees the words 'Top Secret' stamped across something, the first thing one wants to do is have a good gander at it.

My head was spinning as the man went on to ask me questions about my parents.

'We know your father has been in Poland,' he said.

The man was referring to my father, Paul, who was a bio-chemist. Poland was still behind the iron curtain back then, and while employed by a drug company, he'd travelled there for work. The man also asked about my parents' affiliations and politics before suggesting that I go home, discuss all this with them and think carefully about whether I was interested in the position. Yes, I was allowed to tell them about the job, just as long as I didn't do it over the phone. Seriously? Was the college phone really tapped? It all seemed wildly over the top but I thought it best to do as they said, just in case it was and I ended up being shipped off to a small island, never to be heard from again.

As I travelled home my mind was going in all directions. I imagined myself spying in a foreign country, living on my danger money. If I took whatever job it was they were offering I would move country every three years, and I could only ever tell my husband and parents what I was doing. Absolutely nobody else could know.

I wrote to my mother and father in the end, melodramatically advising them to shred and dispose of the letter the very second they'd read it. In the same spirit, Dad wrote back to me instructing me to eat his letter when I'd read it – we all got into the drama of it.

Mum thought it was brilliant. 'You'll meet really interesting people, darling,' she wrote, clearly not taking into consideration that some interesting people might want to waterboard me to extract official secrets.

Dad, on the other hand, was a little more cautious: 'Will you have to kill anyone? Because that's something to think about.'

As much as I loved the idea of all that excitement, in my heart I knew I could never have accepted the position because I could never live a lie. How could I ever have any genuine friendships or get close to people? There would always be a barrier and that, more than anything, turned me off of the idea and I turned them down.

I never really found out for sure why I'd been singled out

to become a spy by MI6, but I heard from a reasonably reliable source that one of my senior tutors at Cambridge was a recruiter who earmarked prospective candidates and pointed them out to the powers-that-be. I couldn't know for sure if that was the reason, but I always thought it had a ring of truth because there was quite a tradition of spies coming from Cambridge. Back then, the secret service was secret and there was no acknowledgment that it even existed. These days it's relatively out in the open with MI6 advertising their positions in *The Times*. There's just no mystery any more, is there?

The bottom line is, I might have been a spy rather than a doctor and my children still love the idea of it.

'How do you know I'm not a spy?' I once asked them. 'I wouldn't be allowed to tell you if I was and if I did tell you, I'd probably have to kill you.'

Post-degree, I ended up working in the City at Andersen Consulting, a huge global management consultancy firm. I chose them because a) they offered the most money and b) because they said they'd send me to Chicago for six weeks for training and I quite fancied that. So, at twenty-one I was seconded to a team working at the London Stock Exchange. But my heart really wasn't in it. In fact, despite making a ton of money I hated every second of being in the City. I didn't like running with the crowd, I hated sitting in dreary meetings and I had a frighteningly low tolerance for all the management bullshit-speak I had to endure on a daily basis. I didn't fit into that world, nor did I want to, and I quickly realized that it wasn't for me. I managed to stick it out for two years, but then it was time to go.

You might be surprised to hear how I decided on my career in medicine. It wasn't something that came to me in a vivid dream or even a true calling to do something worthwhile for humanity – I actually just picked it out of a book. If you were leaving Andersen's they had a rather generous policy known as 'counselling out' where they allowed you a couple of months on full pay to look into what you wanted to do next (I think this was because they realized that a career in management consultancy wasn't for everyone and wanted to help those who were leaving to find their feet again.) Consequently, as I was working in London, I found myself in the University College London careers section for hours on end, trawling through every conceivable option. I ploughed through every folder from A to Z to see what might take my fancy. It wasn't as much roulette as it was pin-the-tail-on-the-donkey, because the truth of it was I had absolutely no idea what I wanted to do. This realization came with a huge amount of anxiety. Why didn't I know? Why didn't I have a vocation? Why wasn't there a burning passion pulling me towards a new and exciting threshold? I didn't know the answer to these questions but after many hours in the careers section, I found myself staring at what seemed like two viable options for someone with my scientific background: veterinarian or doctor. OK, so what now? Maybe I'd have to experience some time looking at both before I decided. That seemed sensible.

First, I went and spent a day with a family friend, a vet who spent an unsettling amount of time in freezing cold fields with his arm up cows' backsides. No. I wasn't going to take any delight in that, in fact it was a hideous day and one that I didn't feel needed revisiting. After that, I spent a day with a GP in Axminster: a lovely man with a small, established practice who, after work, took me to his house where we sat by the fire with his springer spaniels and a gin and tonic each while he recounted absorbing stories about his long career in medicine. Oh yes, I decided, this was much better: warm fires and grateful patients as opposed to subzero fields and cows' arses. Done! Since then, of course, I've considered the idea that I might have had a great day with my vet friend the very next day and a vile time with the doctor, and I can say with some certainty that if that had been the case, I'd have become a vet. There had been no childhood dream about either career, and, on top of that, starting medicine aged twenty-three with absolutely no background or training in it was quite an undertaking. I suppose, if anything, that was what drew me to it: the challenge and the opportunity to do something worthwhile, something that mattered. I loved learning more than anything, and the thing I was and still am best at is academia. I also loved the idea of going back to university and who wouldn't? It was just more years of having no responsibility.

My dad was horrified at the idea of me becoming a student again and not earning, but to be fair I'd managed to save quite a bit of money from my time at Andersen's, and I funded my time at medical school by continuing to work as a free-lance programmer using the skills I'd learnt as a management consultant. Of course, it made things easier that there were no tuition fees back then. I ended up doing an accelerated graduate course at Southampton University, which took four years, and loved it, finally qualifying in 1998 when I was twenty-nine. Quite late, yes, but I think that maturity helped me cope better with the degree, particularly when I was on the wards as a medical student.

## 2

# house rules

ON LEAVING UNIVERSITY, newly qualified doctors were required to do house jobs as the initial part of their training: six months of general medicine followed by another six of general surgery, during which time they could begin to decide in what kind of medicine they'd eventually like to specialize. As it happened, I'd already made that decision, having completed two psychiatry secondments while I was doing my medical degree and loving them both.

But before I could get on with psychiatry training I still had to do my house jobs, starting with the medical rotation in February 1999 on an oncology ward at an acute care hospital. Don't ask me what made me choose oncology from the long list I'd been given at uni, especially since having graduated with honours and a distinction pretty much all options were open to me. Perhaps I imagined it might be more interesting than cardiology or respiratory, I don't know, but ultimately I found it hard going. Most of the time, chemotherapy is given as an outpatient treatment so most of the cancer patients we saw as inpatients were the terminal ones, or people who were struggling with infections because of their treatment. So I ended up spending a lot of my time with patients who subsequently died, which quite often left me feeling helpless.

It's no surprise that people working in an often distressing job develop a kind of defence mechanism, a way of insulating themselves from a grim reality. In a lot of young doctors, it's a dark, sardonic humour that to outsiders probably looks quite callous. Like the so-called 'ash cash'. When a patient died and was due to be cremated, somebody had to sign a form confirming they were definitely dead and that there were no defibrillators, pacemakers, implants or anything metal that might bugger up the cremation burners. The way we earned our ash cash was to go down to the mortuary, take the body from the fridge and then check it for any lurking accoutrements before signing the form. We got something like £18 per form that we signed. Inevitably, if regrettably, a competitive element sprang up as to which department earnt the most ash cash each month. It was invariably us in the oncology department or the respiratory teams who won this rather macabre competition.

Although I'd sort of known there wasn't going to be an awful lot of joy in oncology, the whole thing was quite a rude awakening. I was living in the hospital digs at the time, which was out of necessity more than anything as I spent so much time there, often doing forty-eight-hour shifts at the weekend. I felt very down during that six months and didn't really enjoy it at all.

Being on a ward for the first time can be terrifying for a young doctor. Often, when the senior doctors were off doing clinics, I found myself on my own and the responsibility was intimidating. On one occasion, I was asked to drain a pleural effusion from a woman who had secondary cancer in her lung. I'd had this demonstrated to me, then the second time I was faced with it I was actually doing it – and all on my own. It entails inserting a large needle into the chest to drain off fluid or air that might be collecting. So there I was attempting to complete a tricky, practical procedure on a poor woman with breast cancer, having been shown how to do it just once. God forbid the woman I was performing it on could have read my mind and heard the thoughts running through it: am I going to puncture her lung? Please don't let me hit a nerve or worse still an artery. In that moment, everyone else was busy doing what they had to do and I, as a young doctor, just had to get on with it. Times like that can be quite isolating and I remember feeling very lonely during those first six months out on my own.

There were some brighter times, though, especially when I built a bond with patients who made a lasting impression on me. Aaron was one such patient. He had been diagnosed with non-Hodgkin lymphoma and had to have a great deal of chemotherapy over a long period, so I saw him often and got to know and like him. Aaron was a chatty redhead who enthused about movies and football, usually loudly.

'What do you mean you've not seen *The Matrix*? It's bloody ace!' he'd shout after me. Or, 'I know lots of girls who love football. You want to get yourself down to watch Norwich City. Now *that's* a team!'

He was one of those people who brightened up my workday, and seemed to have an optimistic outlook, despite his disease, so it was devastating to find out that the disease had metastasized and spread to his brain. We knew then that he wasn't going to survive and it was going to be all about management. After that, things changed. Aaron made more and more appearances on the ward because he was frequently fighting off some infection or other, and as the weeks went on he'd have periods of acute confusion because the cancer cells had spread to his brain. During a quiet five minutes one afternoon, I headed over to see him while he was having an antibiotic drip set up.

'I see that rubbish team of yours lost again,' I said.

I was all ready for him to come back at me with some

smart-arse remark, but instead he just looked up me, his eyes filled with tears.

'Are you all right, Aaron?' I said. 'Can I get you anything?'

He opened his mouth to speak, and managed a few slurred words I could barely understand. I half-smiled, not knowing what to say to him, and then noticed that my consultant, Dr Saini, was standing by my side.

'How are you doing today, Aaron?' he said.

Aaron moved his head around, neither a shake nor a nod, and I looked around at Dr Saini, who led me away, seeing my alarm and confusion.

'The brain mets are growing rapidly now, Steph,' he said. 'His speech is severely affected.'

'Is that it, then?' I asked. 'Is there nothing we can do?'

'Well, his steroid dose is high already and we've run out of chemotherapy options. We are just into palliative measures now,' he said.

Aaron was one of the unlucky ones. I suppose we're more accustomed to people having cancer when they're much older, but Aaron was only in his early twenties when he died.

I had another patient called Jessie, a lovely sixteen-year-old girl who had osteosarcoma, which is a bone cancer, and one of the more common types of cancer in teenagers, though it more often affects boys. Jessie had a tumour on her femur and had surgery so the bone could be replaced with metalwork. After that she had to have chemo every four weeks. As her doctor, I'd often sit down and talk with her about how she was coping. It's funny; she was always very upbeat about her disease, but constantly anxious about how her mother was feeling.

I recall one miserably grey, wet afternoon when it was so dark we had to have every light in the ward on, even though it was July. Jessie looked a bit down in the dumps, which wasn't her usual demeanour at all.

'Everything all right, Jessie?' I sat down next to her, glancing up at the bag of chemo medication dripping slowly down a tube and into her right arm. 'Where's your mum today?'

'I didn't want her to come,' she said, matter-of-factly.

'Oh, you've not had a row, have you?'

Jessie looked surprised and shook her head. 'She gets too upset and I can't stand seeing her sad.'

'Well, she's your mum,' I smiled. 'She probably hates you being sick even more than you hate it yourself.'

'Oh, I get that,' she said. 'That's why I'm going to tell her just to drop me off while I have my chemo from now on, so she won't see me being sick or whatever. I don't want her to worry, you know? When I'm home I just try to keep cheerful, so she won't fret.'

I really took to Jessie, not only because she was very sweet but also because she was so open. Most of the teenagers with cancer didn't want to talk. They'd just completely shut down if I asked them how they were. Even if they were doing OK, they clearly didn't want to explore how they were feeling. Jessie was more candid with me, which was surprising given her young age. For her, the hardest thing about having cancer was seeing her mum upset, and after that day she often talked about how it made her feel. She always had to try so hard not to get upset, almost as if she were caring for her mum rather than the other way round. I got to know Jessie well during the course of her treatment, and I'm happy to report that she was one who got better.

Dealing with cancer patients, you can sometimes be thrown a curve ball while trying to solve what should be the simplest of problems. Early on in my time in oncology, I became friendly with a woman called Sally, who had bowel cancer. This began when I was on a night shift and I found her pacing about the ward in agony from constipation, which was a common side effect of her particular chemotherapy but not always an easy thing to sort out. She'd apparently been suffering for a few days, but by then it had become unbearable.

'The doctors want me to have an enema but I can't do that,' she told me.

'Why not?' I said. 'It's quite a simple process, and it seems like it might be a reasonable solution to me.'

'No. I can't,' she said.

Sally had flatly refused any such procedure all day but nobody on the ward had been able to get her to explain why she was so against it. I suspected some of them thought she was just being difficult, but she didn't seem particularly diva-like to me. It turned out to be fortuitous that I'd met Sally on the night shift because it was quiet and I'd had time to talk to her, one on one. I sat with her for a while in one of the side rooms having a cup of chamomile tea and talking about the various side effects of her chemotherapy. The constipation was an ongoing problem and she knew the enema would help but, she told me quietly, she couldn't stand the idea of it and knew it would traumatize her. I didn't push her to tell me why.

Whatever Sally's reasons, I reassured her that I wasn't going to try to persuade her, did what I could for her there and then and headed to my office, pulling out my medical book searching for all the different medications I could think of to ease her constipation. It would have to be some kind of oral medication, and I was determined to find it. After that, I saw Sally frequently and got to know her well. She was in her late fifties and had never had children, so her life had been one of relative solitude and she didn't seem to have a lot of friends. Constipation was a continuing issue throughout her treatment, and I was constantly trying to find ways to ease her discomfort, but I think the best thing I did for Sally was to listen, always taking time to talk to her even if it was at the end of my shift. She was also a good listener and always wanted to know how I was before we turned to how she was doing. In fact, at the end of what was an intense six-month tenure in oncology, we stayed in touch and Sally, to this day, remains the only patient that I ever exchanged numbers with. When I found out that her cancer had spread and was terminal, shortly after I'd left the job, I drove over to her house for a visit.

The two of us spent quite a happy afternoon together, considering her circumstances, but I suppose that was typical of her. She made tea for us both, in prettily painted mugs, and I casually said how attractive they were. Later, as I was putting on my jacket, about to leave, Sally handed me the mugs.

'You should have these,' she said. 'Take them home with you.'

'Really? But they're so nice, don't you want to keep them?' I said.

'I love them too but I'd rather they went to a good home,' she said, smiling. 'I won't need them much longer, will I?'

I had no idea what to say so I took the mugs and hugged

her. I felt pretty upset that such a throwaway comment had prompted Sally to part with something she loved because she knew she was going to die very soon. I put the mugs on the passenger seat of my car and as I drove away I looked down at them, thinking that I was unlikely to return to Sally's house. I was starting a new job at the end of that week, relocating to a smaller county hospital to begin my surgical house job, and so my chances of seeing Sally again were remote.

My next job was as a house officer in breast surgery, which felt far less stressful than oncology. I was much happier. The consultant was a dream and the job was based by the sea so it was all a bit of a relief after the sadness of oncology.

I never did see Sally again. I was at work a few weeks after starting the job when I got a call from her sister to say that Sally had died. I'd never met her sister, but assumed that my phone number was in her book and that she was going through it phoning everybody. Sally's death moved me, perhaps because she was a patient I'd got close to at the start of my career. Sadly, I wasn't able to go to her funeral because I was on call that day, and in a new job I couldn't get the day off – there just wasn't the flexibility.

I've still got one of Sally's mugs. My husband broke the other one, and although it was years later, I still felt a pang of sadness when I threw the pieces into the bin. Of course, he didn't know that it was a precious mug, but he was quite touched when I told him about the time I spent with Sally. I have to confess, I'm always extra careful with the remaining mug.

# 3

# heavy rotation

ONE OF THE THINGS I had enjoyed most about my psychiatry secondments during my medical degree was that I had time to talk to the patients. This was in stark contrast to much of surgery, where there was a conveyer belt of patients coming in for routine day procedures. On a psychiatry ward the patients were in longer term and I could build a relationship with them, which I saw as a positive thing – at least at first. I also found the diagnoses fascinating as well as all the various therapies, and it seemed to me that psychiatrists were an eclectic and welcoming bunch and, on the whole, the most interesting doctors.

So, in February 2000, aged thirty, I ended up on a prestigious and competitive psychiatry rotation. This was to be a three-year Senior House Officer (SHO) rotation, with a different speciality every six months. My first six months was in general adult psychiatry in a large hospital, and my second was in a similar vein but in a smaller outpost. After that, I specialized in old-age psychiatry, and might well have gone on to do forensic psychiatry or psychological therapy if I hadn't cut the whole thing short.

By this time I was renting a lovely little cottage in a tiny village. It was here that I met my husband-to-be, Chris, who owned the local pub – the Trout. I often dropped in on my way home from work, and one night in August 2000 Chris and I just got talking, hitting it off right away. A tall, broad-shouldered ex-rugby player with muscles and jet black hair which was always swept back, Chris had a pair of Oakley sunglasses on top of his head to keep his hair out of his eyes. I had no idea then that he was the pub's owner, instead thinking he was just a talkative barman (I remain gratified to know that I didn't fancy him just because he owned the place). At that time I had a boyfriend who lived in Norway and Chris had a girlfriend, so our first few encounters were nothing more than friendly chats over a glass of red wine on my way home from work.

Unlike working in oncology, I really got my teeth into adult psychiatry, and, as an SHO, I learned a lot – but it was certainly no picnic. I was often charged with deciding whether to release patients who might be a risk to themselves, or others, and that was quite a responsibility. The job taught me how to make thorough determinations about levels of risk, which was to come in very useful down the line, but I sometimes found it overwhelming.

Working an afternoon in an outpatient clinic, seeing six or seven severely depressed patients back-to-back, can be quite depleting. I've always thought of myself as the kind of doctor who gives something of herself to the patient, chiefly because I think that's what being a doctor is. In an outpatient clinic, a psychiatrist might have twenty minutes to half an hour sitting with a patient while they talk about how things are. Often psychiatrists use that time to echo back what the patient has said and then try to help them come up with strategies to deal with their difficulties. I always wanted to show empathy and build up a therapeutic relationship with my patients. I didn't want people to feel as if there was some kind of glass wall between them and me. Unfortunately, this approach to my patients had a downside and came at quite a cost to myself; dealing with what was often deep despair in patients I was trying to help, I'd find myself thinking about them long after our meetings and sometimes I felt like it was impossible to switch off. I'd be lying in the bath thinking, what can I say to stop Patient X from taking his life? How can I make Patient Y see that she will get better?

My Patient X was Simon, a young man who was studying

for a PhD in history at a London university. Simon was severely underweight in a way that reflected his self-neglect and deep unhappiness – and when I say unhappiness I mean serious unhappiness. He was suicidal but super-bright, so not the sort of person I could just hand out platitudes to about how beautiful life could be. As well as being deeply depressed, he also had a borderline personality disorder, that made him quite manipulative, so I was never sure if what he was telling me was true or simply to elicit a reaction. Like many people with a personality disorder, he needed masses of attention but had an eggshell-fragile ego to boot, taking offence at the slightest remark. I think you probably get the picture: Simon was a difficult patient and gave me a lot of sleepless nights because when he said ‚he was going to commit suicide he sounded like he meant it.

Yes, Simon was that person whom I would go home and think about endlessly. How could I help him? How could I turn such devastating pessimism around? There was a lovely person inside. A good, intelligent, useful person, and I wanted to help him get better and fulfil all that potential. As time went on, things got even worse. He hardly bathed and his hair was a lank, stinking mess, but I knew his objectionable appearance was a manifestation of how he felt about himself. I got that.

By the time I started treating him, he'd been in hospital for ages and had missed a good year of his PhD, but eventually the combination of therapy and medication meant that there was a possibility he'd be able to resume his normal life. I hoped Simon would eventually be discharged from hospital and go back to university to continue the work he'd started – but he had other ideas.

'There's no point; they won't take me back. I've been away too long and they won't care about the whys and wherefores.'

'That's simply not true, Simon,' I said. 'There's absolutely no way they wouldn't take your mental health into consideration. Look, why don't I arrange to take you to talk to your supervisor there? As your doctor they'll have to listen to me, I'm sure.'

'We can try but I don't think it'll help,' he said.

Everything was a struggle with Simon, but I did manage to arrange a meeting with his PhD supervisor, emphasizing how important it was for Simon's mental wellbeing for him to finish the work he'd started and for it not to have been a waste. At the meeting, his supervisor was extremely encouraging, assuring me that he'd love to have Simon back.

I felt that I'd moved heaven and earth to help Simon but, whatever I did, it was never good enough: he still told me on a regular basis that he wanted to kill himself. I carried on doing everything I could to help him but it was energy-sapping. He was still regularly running off to Tesco to try to buy tablets on which to overdose; it became almost like a game, repeated over and over. By then I wasn't even convinced he really wanted to die, but it was simply the only way he could express how shitty he felt.

I spent hours of my time wondering if his threats of suicide were a cry for attention, but as his doctor I could never assume that. Then on one visit to my practice, he surprised me with an announcement.

'I'm going to ask my girlfriend Amber to marry me when she comes to see me tonight,' he said. 'Isn't that amazing?'

I knew about Amber, although I'd never met her and hadn't realized their relationship was all that serious – so the declaration of impending nuptials threw me somewhat.

'Oh, well yes, that is good, Simon,' I said, wondering what might happen if she turned him down. Would that finally push him over the edge?

'It's great that you're actually looking to the future,' I added, but he looked away as if he didn't really want to acknowledge that aspect of it.

'Let's see what she says,' Simon said, seriously.

I wondered if he might be testing Amber. There's an element in some people with a personality disorder that compels them to continually test the people around them; pushing them away to see just how far they can be pushed. Success in doing so will then confirm their belief that they are unlovable.

I decided to acknowledge Simon's marriage proposal as a

46

positive thing, and he did indeed ask her. Amber, sensibly, told him that she would love to marry him but that they should wait until he was better and out of hospital. He actually took it quite well, but I had serious doubts that he'd ever fully recover because of his personality disorder. All I could hope was that he'd eventually learn to manage it better. That was my one hope for Simon because antidepressants were never going to work for somebody like him. Sadly, I never got to see any significant improvement in him before I left the hospital. Simon had been an inpatient for the entire six months I was there, and he was still there when my rotation ended.

During that year, I spent so much time ruminating on both my inpatients and my outpatients that it was slowly but surely engulfing me, and although I wasn't yet living with Chris, he was often there when I got a phone call at two in morning and had to head off to the hospital because I was on call. Occasionally, I'd confide in him about how worried I'd been about a certain patient, so most of the time when I disappeared into the night, he'd lie awake waiting for me to come home again – already quite protective of me, despite it being early in our relationship. I guess he could see how stressful the job was.

After two stints of six months on rotation, it came to that point where I was going to have to start preparing for my exams for entry to the Royal College of Psychiatrists, because in medicine that is the only way to progress in your field. I'd now done three years at Cambridge followed by four years of medical school, and as much as I loved academia, the thought of doing any more exams filled me with dismay. I knew that if I stayed on in psychiatry, I was headed for more studying and exam after exam until I became a consultant, and that wasn't what I wanted. As far as learning was concerned, I was all burned out.

So as I watched and listened to my colleagues planning their futures and studying for their exams, that little part of me that always longed to be different pushed its way to the surface again. Like some kind of career gypsy, I couldn't seem to settle on one single thing and whenever the people around me expected me to stick to one particular path, I always felt compelled to take another. Even though I'd already started my next rotation in old-age psychiatry, I just couldn't see myself going through that sausage factory: house officer, SHO, registrar and consultant. I could never do it when I was working in the City and now I'd found that I couldn't do it in medicine either. So I made the decision to leave. I didn't really discuss it with Chris or my parents or even very much with my employers. It was just something I knew I had to do for my own sanity; I had to start looking for another job. There was just one small problem . . . I had no idea what I actually wanted to do. Again.

# 4

# a dead end?

'LOOK, STEPHANIE, I can accept that you're burnt out and that you don't want to do any more exams, but I'm not convinced this is the right job for you. In fact, if you were offered it, I'd insist that you didn't stay for very long. This would merely be a stop-gap.'

It was an unusually bright morning in January 2001, and there I was on the phone to a no-nonsense gentleman called Dr Crosby, opening and closing my mouth like a fish while trying to get a word in edgeways. I'd just downed my third cup of morning Java perched at my kitchen table where, exactly one week earlier, I'd held aloft a freshly printed (and, I thought, rather impressive) CV, ready to take on the world. That morning, I'd felt proud to be someone who didn't feel the need to follow the crowd, proud to be somebody who was marching to the beat of her own drum. But now? After this phone call? Maybe my drumbeat was a little out of sync.

'Dr Crosby, I actually think . . .'

'I do know what I'm talking about, Stephanie,' he said.

'But . . .'

It was a tricky point for me to argue, to be honest. I actually had no idea what the post of 'Port Medical Officer at Heathrow Airport' might entail. It was a cocktail of intrigue and a desperate need to shake things up that had drawn me to the unobtrusive advert in the *British Medical Journal* a week or so earlier. The *BMJ* is where most medical jobs are advertised in their various categories: General Practice, Ophthalmology, Urology, Renal Medicine, and so on. At the end of all the fancy stuff, there's a tiny little section entitled 'Other'. It's where all the weird, oddball, unclassifiable medical jobs lurk. Like this one.

It wasn't just curiosity, though. The idea of working at Heathrow really lit a fire in me. Ever since I was little I'd loved airports. The idea of whizzing off somewhere glamorous, or even unglamorous, was always so exciting to me, and if anyone we knew was taking a plane trip, even our neighbours or relatives we didn't much care for, my mum and I would make the effort to go and see them off. As a child, I was thrilled by the buzz: the security checks, the roar of the engines, the duty-free shops. Who wouldn't want to work in a place like that? It was intoxicating; a step into the unknown. This job was just what I needed, wasn't it?

'Are you listening, Stephanie?'

As far as filling the Heathrow position went, the buck stopped with Dr Crosby. I'd hoped, that morning, to come off the phone puffed-up with enthusiasm, nay, excitement about this prospective position, but in reality the opposite happened. Rather than telling me what a thrilling opportunity the job might be, he was strangely condemnatory.

'I'm serious. This really isn't any sort of decent career path and you should simply view it as a temporary move.'

There was that phrase: career path. Doctors are notoriously obsessed with career paths, by which they mean a trajectory towards becoming a consultant or perhaps a GP. A consultant himself, Dr Crosby didn't actually work at Port Health, Heathrow, but was the doctor responsible for it within the local authority, and seemed fixed on the idea that taking the position could mess up my career royally if I wasn't careful. The role at Heathrow was what's known as a non-training post, in that it wasn't on the career path to anywhere in particular. And I know that Dr Crosby had genuine concerns about my career stalling before it really got going.

However, I was already well aware how hard it would be to stay on the path towards becoming a consultant, particularly as a woman who one day wanted a family. I think that's why so many women go into general practice, where it's possible to work three days a week. When you're on a rotation six months at a time, here, there and everywhere, you're moving hospitals, specialities and sometimes homes, and you're working five days plus one weekend a month on call, and a night during the week on call. The exam process for entry into any royal college, which is what is required to become a consultant, is also brutal. Split into two parts, basic and specialized, there's a lot of work involved and I just wasn't willing for my life to be subsumed into medicine to that extent and, if I did have a family, never to see them.

'It's an unusual job and a bit of a dead end one if you want the truth,' Dr Crosby went on. 'I accept that sometimes one has an urge to step off the treadmill and try something different, of course I do, but if your interview does go well, and I see no reason why it shouldn't, I think we would need to put a cap on how long you should stay there. I would suggest a year and that's it.'

'Oh. OK.'

I was baffled at the time, but things became a little clearer at the interview a week or so later.

Ah yes! The interview. Not exactly my finest moment in the medical profession, it has to be said. It took place in Hillingdon town centre at the nondescript administrative offices of Hillingdon Health Authority. I might have taken the fact that

# a dead end?

I crashed my car into the back of a double decker bus en route there as some kind of sign from the universe that this might not be the right path. Luckily, I was neither injured nor did I injure anyone else, in fact the worst of it was that it wasn't even my own car I'd propelled into a bus, it was Chris's. Still, it wasn't totalled and the bus came out of it unscathed so I wasn't charged with any sort of driving offence, but the shock of it meant that rather than appearing as a vision of composed serenity when I arrived in front of the small panel for the interview, I was in fact rather discomfited and unfocused.

On the panel, Dr Crosby was flanked by another male doctor, plus an iron-haired lady who didn't exactly look like she was ready to be dazzled by me or anyone else, ever. It wasn't as though I expected the interview to be especially challenging. This kind of job was quite low down on the health authority's interest level. They were much more concerned with what was going on under their noses at the hospitals and clinics. This position was tucked away at Heathrow Airport and very much an 'out of sight, out of mind' situation: not on the radar and not mainstream. To be honest, I got the impression that it was all a bit of a bother for these people to have to interview me at all, and consequently the interview was suitably short and perfunctory.

Well, I say that. I still managed to screw up some of my answers to their questions quite comprehensively. For instance, when the iron-haired lady asked me what infectious diseases I thought we might be checking for at Heathrow, my mind went utterly blank.

'Oh! Well . . .' I actually had no idea so I offered up the first thing that came into my head. 'Hepatitis? Er . . . A, B and C?'

Talk about showing my ignorance. Hepatitis B and C, both transferred by blood and bodily fluids, are not at all what they'd be checking for at Heathrow. The panel all looked back at me as if to say, you really haven't got a clue, have you? And there was no arguing with that. I can't remember exactly what sort of preparation I'd done for the interview, but it clearly wasn't enough. I assumed it was because, academically, I looked pretty good on paper that I was offered the post. I mean, I'd been to Cambridge, I had two degrees including a medical degree with honours – I was a catch, wasn't I? Or perhaps the truth of my appointment lay in the fact that nobody else had applied for the position. Prospective candidates were probably too put off by Dr Crosby's bleak vision to have taken it any further than an initial enquiry. Either way, I bagged the job. And stayed for eleven years.

# access all areas

I DON'T REMEMBER having any specific nerves as I left the house for my first day as a Heathrow doctor, possibly due to the fact that I still had scant knowledge of what I was actually supposed to be doing once I got there. Honestly, I was winging it, and despite the fact that nobody I'd told about the job seemed to quite get it either, I was at least spurred on by my mother's shared enthusiasm about me working in an airport – she loved them as much as I did. However I had one immediate problem. Even though I'd technically had the job for one month, I wasn't actually allowed inside the airport because I hadn't been given security clearance yet. A doctor working at Port Health has to have the equivalent of an 'Access All Areas' pass – a red badge which allows us to go airside, which means the section of the airport terminal beyond

Passport Control. In fact, there was nowhere in the airport I couldn't go, which is why this sort of clearance was so hard and took so long to get – lots of forms, lots of questions, lots of everything. It meant that I had almost a month on full pay without actually doing anything.

Despite this unexpected lull, it had been a busy few weeks leading up to that first morning. I'd handed in my notice at work, leaving with good wishes from my new team in old-age psychiatry – whom I'd left in the lurch somewhat, truth be told – and I'd moved into Chris's cottage, which felt wonderful. In fact, if I was ever going to use that rather hackneyed phrase, 'it was the start of a whole new era', this would have been the time. Not that I got off to an encouraging start, though – my car conked out before I even got to Heathrow, and I had to wait an hour for the AA to come and start its engine. Unbelievable! After all that hanging around, waiting to start my shiny new role, I had to phone one of the DOs and tell her that I was going to be late because I'd broken down on the M4. Now I was stressed. Good job I didn't take it as an omen for my future career.

The biggest win of that first day was that I liked my boss. Well, you never know, do you? He might have been some authoritarian horror and then what? Wasn't it enough that I'd taken this strange fork in my career – becoming a doctor who works and sleeps at Heathrow Airport – without having to answer to somebody I didn't like? Dr Thanabalasingham (Dr Thana for short) was Sri Lankan, about twenty-five years older than me and a proud family man. He clearly loved talking about his two daughters, who were both bright and incredibly engaged with education (and who both went on to be high-achieving medical professionals themselves: one a doctor, the other a dentist). As well as that, his wife was an ear, nose and throat doctor, so these days they have all medical bases pretty much covered as a family. Even on that first day, Dr Thana struck me as a warm, supportive man and I'm happy to say that never changed throughout our time working together and continues even to this day.

On my first morning at HCU, he showed me how to identify pulmonary TB on a chest X-ray. It's a bacterial infection affecting the lungs which can also spread to other organs. You can catch TB by breathing in air droplets from a cough or sneeze of an infected person, and it's spread by prolonged close contact with a sufferer. It's not something doctors are used to seeing in the UK because these days it's usually only seen in certain groups: immigrants from countries with high incidences of TB, prison populations, drug users, the homeless and people with diseases that affect their immune system, like HIV. In 2001–2 there were just over 13,000 cases of TB in the UK, but between 1851 and 1910, nearly four million people are said to have died from it in England and Wales. Many of you will remember the dreaded BCG injection we were all given at secondary school to vaccinate us against it, but even that's no longer routinely given. It was replaced in 2005 with a targeted programme for babies, children and young adults at higher risk. This drop in TB rates over the years was mostly related to improvements in housing, nutrition and access to treatment, but in less developed countries these things are still an issue and so TB rates remain higher – and that's where we come in.

Having come from a background of psychiatry, I probably wouldn't have recognized it on an X-ray from a vase of tulips before Dr Thana showed me that morning, but diagnosing TB was to become one of the main components of my work at Port Health.

On an X-ray the lungs, which are full of air, show up as black because they let through the most radiation, while more solid things like ribs attenuate the X-rays, letting fewer through, so they show up as white. Healthy lungs should appear dark with the white shadows of the ribs clearly seen in contrast. The heart is in the middle, which also shows as white because, like ribs, it attenuates the X-rays. Dr Thana explained that I should be looking at each lung for any lesions which were pale against the usual dark of the lung tissue and which might indicate TB. Faint and diffuse shadows indicate more recent, active disease, and bright white lesions mean that calcification has occurred, which happens when a person had TB, some time ago. So if someone has bright white spots or patches, it's old TB, and if it's a shadow like a little patch of soft cloud, it's more likely an active infection. The active infection is the one that concerns us more because it hasn't been walled in by the body's immune system, and is contagious.

'Miliary tuberculosis is the most serious,' Dr Thana said. 'That's when both lungs will have widespread coverage with tiny pale patches of disease due to blood-borne spread of the bacteria. Miliary TB can be fatal, so people with that need to be hospitalized. It's rare and we don't see it very often, but it's certainly not unheard of.'

He showed me how to check the root of the lungs, the hila, where blood vessels come from the heart into the lungs. Here there are lymph nodes and if they are enlarged it can be a sign of TB.

'You have to look at the X-ray systematically,' Dr Thana said. 'First you look at the trachea to see if it's deviated from one side to the other, because that might indicate various conditions. Then you look at the heart shadow. Is the heart enlarged? Is it normal? Then you look at the hila and then the lung fields. Try to be systematic about it because that way you won't miss anything.'

It was a fair amount to take in at one go, and I'd never have guessed that after I'd been at HCU a couple of years I could literally flick through chest X-rays. It's basically pattern recognition and anyone can be taught to do it. At Heathrow, we had a brilliant digital system where we could reverse the colouring – so everything that was white turned dark and vice versa – and we could also zoom in for maximum precision, which would help us spot smaller lesions. We might also identify other conditions that the passenger was unaware of, like dextrocardia. In Latin, *dexter* means 'right'. Dextrocardia is a condition in which the apex of the heart is located on the right rather than the usual left. Obviously, if a person isn't aware they have dextrocardia it's always worth informing them, although the condition doesn't endanger them. We could also detect things like a collapsed lung, or even what we thought might be lung cancer, and for those patients we would arrange follow-up appointments at Hillingdon or Northwick Park hospitals.

It was perhaps because I wasn't all that much older than his eldest daughter that my relationship with Dr Thana often felt quite paternal, and I recall him crowing like a proud father the first time I nailed the diagnosis of active TB correctly.

There was a whole myriad of staff in Port Health, and at first it was hard to get my head around the machinations of it all. There were doctors, radiographers, HCOs, and DOs, and each terminal had its very own cast list. The HCOs were there to support the medical staff, input passenger information and assist on flights whenever doctors attended. The DOs were in charge of them. There wasn't a doctor at Terminals 1 and 2, but they were both always staffed with HCOs. In Terminal 3, which was the busiest as far as Port Health was concerned, there was a doctor plus a pair of HCOs and a DO. The Terminal 3 doctors worked a 7am-7pm shift when they also oversaw anything going on in Terminals 1 and 2, because they were all in the Central Terminal Area. In Terminal 4 there was another doctor and two more HCOs, and when Terminal 5 opened in 2008, the doctor at Terminal 4 oversaw any medical matters there. The Terminal 4 doctors worked a twenty-four hour shift and covered the whole airport during the night.

I was quite surprised to find that there were a few doctors who seemed to have been at Heathrow since the dawn of time, like Dr Abbot, who was sort of second-in-command after Dr Thana. She was a smart, austere woman who'd previously worked abroad, so her knowledge was excellent and, by the time I arrived, she had the system totally sussed and was completely in control of her work schedule. Like Dr Thana, she did three split shifts a week in Terminal 3, no nights or weekends, and down the line I often took over from her when she went home at 7pm. In my first few weeks there I made the grave mistake of asking if she'd mind swapping a shift with me, and if looks could have killed . . .

'I don't do swaps,' she snapped, and that was the end of the conversation.

Still, Dr Abbot was a good teacher and always a good person to ask if you needed to know something, despite her rather ascetic manner.

Later that first day, at Dr Thana's suggestion, I ventured out of Terminal 3 and headed over to Terminal 4 where I'd be based much of the time. In fact, this was where I'd be sleeping whenever I was on a twenty-four-hour shift – my new home from home, so to speak. The duty doctor there that day was Dr Sood, an Indian man with a welcoming smile who told me right off the bat that absolutely nothing was going to happen for the next three or four hours, until the evening flights, so I'd be better getting acquainted with the layout of the airport.

'I suppose that makes sense,' I said. 'But I should have a look at where I'm going to be working and sleeping first.'

Dr Sood smiled and nodded. 'Indeed! You're going to be spending a lot of time here, Dr Green.'

Beyond the front desk was a long corridor of cubicles where patients could get undressed, ready for X-rays or examination. Further down the corridor was the X-ray room, which was white and pristine, all very high-tech with a brand-new, low-radiation X-ray machine, and on from that was a rest room for the HCOs who worked there. In contrast, this was old and dark with 1970s furniture. At the end of the corridor I came to what would soon be my little office – a sort of time-share with the other HCU doctors – which was full of shelves crammed with crusty, old books. I then walked through another door that led to the doctors' sleeping quarters, which was cold comfort farm to say the least. Like the rest of Terminal 4's HCU, the small bedroom had no windows – so I would be hermetically sealed in. In one corner, there was a tiny, single bed with a little bedside table and one of those tortuously uncomfortable hospital chairs with a bar that cuts into the lower back. The 'en suite' bathroom beyond had a nasty, old bath that I could never see myself using, a basin, a loo and a 1970s hand-held shower that promised little more than a polite dribble at best. It was featureless and grim, with not a scrap of high street art or even a tacky ornament in sight; nothing, in fact, to render it in the slightest bit homely or comfortable. It was all very depressing and I made a quick exit, telling myself that I'd only ever spend time there if I were asleep or using the bathroom.

'Now you should go to each terminal and find out how you get airside,' Dr Sood said as I came back into the office, where he was checking an X-ray. 'That will be the best use of your time on your first day. I'll give you a map, but each terminal is different so it can be tricky.'

He wasn't kidding. When the public come into a terminal at Heathrow, they're met by an array of shops and eateries, but trust me there's a whole world going on behind the scenes, and I had to find out how to get into this magical kingdom via all the available portals, both on foot and by car.

Each terminal had control posts around the perimeter fence for staff arriving by car, and also control posts within the terminals that took staff from landside to airside if they were arriving on foot. They were there to make the same checks on staff as were made on passengers when they travel from landside to airside, to stop anyone taking weapons and other nasties anywhere near the planes.

The control posts were, as Dr Sood helpfully informed me, in different locations in each terminal. And to complicate things further, the control posts inside the terminals were always moving when maintenance work was going on. The location of the portals seemed to change with alarming regularity, so I might have three days off work and come back to find that someone had done a sneaky refit and the secret door had been moved without anyone telling me.

The posts along the perimeter fence worked like an airlock. When I drove through one gate it closed behind me, leaving me in a sort of no-man's-land where any bags I was carrying had to go through a scanner, just as any passenger's bag would. I had to get out of the car for it to be checked and go through a metal detector just as I would if I were arriving on foot. Only once I'd been cleared would the second door or gate of the control post open, and finally I would be airside.

Down the line it became it became an utter nuisance, especially after the 100ml law came in for liquids in 2006.

Yes, that even applied to those of us working at the airport and it took me a while to get my head around it. I lost a lot of stuff in the first few weeks of that law: moisturizer, yoghurt, milk, shower gel, shampoo. I was forever in Boots replacing my life's little necessities.

While irritating, this constant movement and change was also what made Heathrow exciting. There was an amazing buzz the whole time and an extraordinary energy about the place; so very different to being in a hospital where the atmosphere can sometimes wear you down. But even on quiet days I loved being at the airport. I still got a kick from the beating pulse of Heathrow.

I didn't know it then, but my first evening stint in Terminal 3, later that week, was a measure of stranger things to come. Most of that day had been fairly routine: getting to grips with the various forms I might be required to issue and checking between sixty and a hundred X-rays for TB – nothing out of the ordinary. Things really kicked off with a phone call from a member of the Heathrow staff at around 10.30pm.

'We have a lady from a flight from Botswana here whose brother hasn't come out of the toilet,' he said. 'She's in the immigration hall.'

'Did she not go in to look for him?' I asked.

'No, she came and alerted me,' he said. 'We're going to have to go in and find him, so could you be here on standby?'

Here we go.

This had happened in Terminal 3, so I was at the scene in less than a minute, discovering the aforementioned lady – a smart, black woman in her early fifties – quite overwrought with worry, just outside the public toilets. Inside, a burly shaven-headed security officer was getting ready to open up the cubicle while his colleague, to whom I'd spoken on the telephone, stood outside, making sure no one else came in. Airport security staff were issued with a bunch of keys that could open any of the cubicles, so there was no need for any strong-arm stuff.

The officer looked around at me as I came into the toilets and I noticed the sweat on his forehead.

'I'm Dr Green,' I said.

'My name is Joseph,' he said. 'I've just started working here today.'

'Well, that makes two of us,' I said, smiling. 'How long has he been in there, Joseph?'

He gave me a worried, sideways glance. 'Quite a while, and he's not responding to calls through the door so I'm opening it up.'

He chewed his lip nervously, probably thinking what I was; that this wasn't looking good.

'All right, let's get in there,' I said.

Joseph unlocked the door and pulled it open, with me right behind him.

'Shit!' He jumped back while I looked in over his shoulder.

The man was slumped on the toilet, clearly dead and almost naked. His jacket and one of his shoes were on the floor, his shirt was undone and hanging off, and his trousers and underwear were down around his ankles. For some reason, the man had been in the midst of stripping off his clothes as he died.

'OK, I wasn't expecting that,' I said.

The dead man was a little older than his sister, probably early sixties, and while looking at him I ran through the likely causes of sudden death in my mind: a pulmonary embolism or maybe a heart attack. His eyes were open, full of fear, and the chaos of his situation suggested a scene of frantic desperation. This was something that had overtaken him quite quickly and unexpectedly. I stepped inside the cubicle and followed the protocols. I felt his pulse, listened for a heartbeat and shone a light in his eyes as we always have to, even when it's pretty clear a person is dead. After that I recorded his death and headed out of the toilets to break the news to the man's sister, while Joseph secured the area. It was a fairly tragic start to my new job, but also a puzzling one. Why on earth would this man have stripped off like that in a tiny cubicle in an airport loo?

I wasn't the only one baffled by this either. As Joseph and his colleague led the man's tearful sister away to a quiet room, an Immigration Officer (IO) arrived on the scene, eager to get some answers.

'What do you think happened, Dr Green? Why is he undressed?'

He was putting me on the spot, especially without a post-mortem, but somewhere in the deep recesses of my medical training I thought I remembered that hypoxia, which is lack of oxygen to the brain, can sometimes cause people to undress themselves. That was right, wasn't it? It's a reaction to the terrifying sensation of not having enough oxygen to breathe; people have been known to tear clothes off themselves. Yes, hypoxia, possibly due to a pulmonary embolism or a heart attack. It was the only explanation for the undressing that I could come up with.

The bemused IO looked me up and down as I offered this explanation. 'So you don't think there's anything suspicious about the fact he was practically naked then?'

'I wouldn't have thought so,' I said. 'I mean, he was alone in the cubicle, wasn't he? What possible reason would he have to get undressed? I think he had a heart attack or a clot to the lung and loosened his tie and shirt in his confusion.'

The man's body was taken away for a postmortem, and although I couldn't be 100 per cent certain I was right, I'd pretty much settled on my theory. Back in my office, I read up on undressing while dying, just to be sure. There it was in black and white . . . *hypothermia!* I read on. *'Hypothermia sufferers often undress before they die. The phenomenon of taking your clothes off when freezing to death is called "paradoxical undressing", and it's an extremely common behaviour for people dying of hypothermia.'*

*Not* hypoxia then. Hypothermia. OK, so that was an easy mistake to make, right? Apparently, paradoxical undressing happens in between 20 and 50 per cent of cases of severe hypothermia. Now I felt a bit of an idiot. I mean, it was highly unlikely that this poor guy had frozen to death in that little toilet cubicle. Perhaps I'd just keep quiet about this and wait for the postmortem result.

An hour later, Dr Thana called me from home.

'So, how are you faring on your first twenty-four-hour-shift, Stephanie? Everything OK?'

'It's been interesting to say the least, Dr Thana.'

'How so?'

'Well, breaking into a cubicle in the men's toilets to recover a half-naked body wasn't something I was expecting,' I said.

He fell silent for a second, so I filled him in on the details.

'That certainly is quite something on your first day.' He sounded solemn as my regaling of the event came to an end. 'But you know . . . I think you'll find there will be plenty more like that to come and you'll get used to it.'

At 11.30pm, I headed from Terminal 3 to Terminal 4, as

ready as I could be for my very first night sleeping in an air-port. As I approached the front desk, the HCOs on duty both stood up to greet me: a well turned-out blonde and a woman my own age with short, dark hair.

'How's your first day been?' the smart blonde said.

'Oh you know, weird,' I said. 'I think it's going to take a bit of getting used to, that's for sure.'

She nodded. 'I heard what happened over in Terminal 3. You're Dr Green, aren't you?'

'Yes, Stephanie,' I said.

'I'm Megan,' she said. 'I expect we're going to be seeing a lot of one another. And this is Sarah.'

'Good to meet you, Stephanie,' Sarah said. Her face opened into a lovely smile, which made her face crinkle. 'Can I get you a cup of tea?'

'I'd love that, thank you.'

Twenty minutes later I lay in bed, thinking how friendly the HCOs had been, how friendly everyone had been so far. OK, so maybe the job was a bit out of the ordinary but at least the people were nice. That first night turned out to be a quiet one, and I have to admit I was relieved. Don't get me wrong, it's not that I wasn't looking forward to a challenge and a bit of adventure, but there's only so much excitement a girl can take on her first twenty-four-hour shift. On top of that I was absolutely knackered – asleep within minutes.

Dr Crosby had been right about one thing; this was going to be an unusual job; one that nobody outside the airport even really knew about. In fact it was unlike any other medical job in the UK, or even the world, because, as far as I know, most airports – including the other airports in the UK – don't have a permanent doctor on the port, they just call a doctor in if needed. These days, even the Heathrow Port Health is limited, operating only from 7am to 10pm, but for the eleven years I was there it was staffed twenty-four hours a day, seven days a week. And it was non-stop.

# 6

# hidden cargo

IN THE FIRST FEW WEEKS of the job, I discovered a big
upside to being a Port Health doctor: I wasn't feeling that
familiar drag of patients who kept coming back and never
got better. My work on psychiatry and oncology rotations
had meant regularly seeing the same patients over and again,
knowing that many of them couldn't be cured. At HCU, I
did everything I could for a patient while they were there,
and then I handed them over to whoever was going to give
ongoing care: paramedics, the local hospital or Immigration.
I rarely if ever saw them again. My next patient was always
going to be somebody new. It was an ever-changing flow and
an ever-changing picture and, after my previous medical incar-
nations with the weight of getting to know so many people,
it was a relief.

Port Health's jurisdiction extended only to the airside area, and then only to Arrivals; it was not concerned with passengers leaving the country, only those entering. If anything happened in the baggage hall, or Departures, for instance, it was nothing to do with me or any of the other staff at HCU.

The job itself had two parts, which were governed by two separate Acts of Parliament. One was the Immigration Act of 1971, and for me that meant supporting Immigration: making decisions on people who had, or appeared to have, medical or psychiatric problems, estimating the cost of possible care if they came into the country and identifying any medication they might be carrying, so as to pinpoint any unseen conditions they might have and what the ramifications might be if they required treatment in the UK.

Our work on TB diagnosis came under the Immigration Act too. This was probably the largest part of my role because anyone coming into the UK for more than six months from a country where TB was endemic, say on a work or student visa or as an immigrant, had to be X-rayed, and there were X-ray machines at every terminal. The six month cut-off might seem strange as someone could feasibly pass on TB after a week of being in the country, but a line had to be drawn somewhere or the number of X-rays would simply be unmanageable. If an incoming passenger brought a recent chest X-ray that clearly came from a hospital and confirmed they were healthy, that was also acceptable, although we had to be careful because there was quite a black market in 'clear' X-rays in certain territories. Sometimes they were of such poor quality I couldn't see what the hell was going on, and at other times an X-ray would have a date on it but no name, so it might have been a snapshot of any old bones. It was well known to us that in parts of some countries you could pick and choose your X-rays from an array of different ones, all hanging up on a stall like a row of tea towels, so these we treated with a degree of scepticism. On more than one occasion I had men present me with X-rays on which I could clearly see the breast shadow of a woman. It was a potential minefield, so one had to be thorough.

As well as the radiographer who took the X-rays, we also had a consultant radiologist – a doctor who specialized in reading them. Dr Gallagher was a tall, slender, experienced doctor who usually wore a tweed skirt with a jacket and a plain blouse. She was actually a retired consultant who did it for fun, but she was a formidable intellect and I was a bit in awe of her. She would quality-control our reporting, coming in once a week and taking a random day's X-ray samples. For instance, she might come in to review Wednesday's X-rays on the system, and whichever doctors were on that day would be under the scrutiny of her beady eye. She'd trawl through all the X-rays, cross-checking her reporting with ours to ensure we hadn't missed anything, and then report any discrepancies in what I thought of as the Book of Shame. I was always nervous when she'd been in because she always included the name of the doctor who'd made the error, so that we could learn from our mistakes. It was all about quality control and ensuring the accuracy of our reporting. At first it was daunting to have one's work scrutinized in such detail, but Dr Gallagher would always find time to have a kind word with anyone who had missed something significant. Her wealth of knowledge was fantastic and she was a good teacher. Though she terrified me in those first few months, I really liked her once I got to know her – perhaps because I always had a low failure rate, well below the unit average of reporting errors.

The rest of our work was governed by the Public Health (Aircraft) Regulations Act of 1979 under which we had a duty to prevent danger to the public health from incoming aircraft. This second part of the job entailed our boarding any incoming flight where there was sickness or death on board, chiefly to ascertain the risk to public health, giving us significant authority. If I boarded a flight I had jurisdiction not just over the passengers, but over the whole flight including the crew and even the pilots. It was quite a responsibility and something I learned on the job. At the same time we had a duty to the airlines to minimize disruption, which meant that we had to do whatever had to be done very quickly – there was no time for rumination and planning. Time was money and that was always a pressure.

One of my early allies at Port Health was a radiographer called Jane Knight. Jane was about fifteen years older than me, with brown bobbed hair, a big chest and a kind face. She dressed with comfort in mind, always in flat shoes teamed with her radiographer's dress, which was white with a red collar and red piping. Like me, Jane had rejected the norm, striving to do something different in her career. At a young age, she went to work in Labrador, part of the Canadian province of Newfoundland and quite remote. There she'd spent four months at a place called Happy Valley Hospital, a Mission Hospital looking after indigenous Eskimos and Indians among whom pulmonary TB was rife. It was a single-handed post and if any equipment needed fixing, she had to do it herself following telephone instructions from an engineer in St John's, hundreds of kilometres away.

A clearly resilient woman, Jane had two grown-up children she'd raised alone, her husband having died when they were very young. Jane and I were paired together on several of my early shifts at Heathrow and our friendship was sealed over the *Telegraph* cryptic crossword, which she kindly taught me how to do whenever we had a quiet half-hour. On a 7am till 7pm shift in Terminal 3, the work tended to dry up for a few hours from about ten in the morning because there weren't many flights coming in, and those that did were the ones from Europe or the US, which never generated much work for us. This was when Jane and I would sit and put the world to rights, and she would patiently oversee the honing of my cryptic crossword skills.

You might think that all sounds like a bit of a breeze, but trust me, the hours between 7pm and midnight more than made up for it.

On what had been an unusually quiet day during my first month, a flustered young IO tore into the unit while I sat with Jane, wrestling with an impossible 15 across.

'Someone has just collapsed outside the toilets in the immigration hall, Dr Green.'

We both looked up from the newspaper. What was it about the toilets in the immigration hall? What was it this time?

'Have you called the paramedics?' I said.

There was always a team of paramedics on standby at the airport, although not based with us in HCU.

'I don't think so,' the IO said. 'This guy went down on his knees and then just sort of laid down on the floor. He's conscious but very distressed. I haven't called paramedics yet.'

'OK, take me to him . . . sorry, what's your name?'

'Jack,' he said.

'OK, take me to him, Jack.'

I jumped up, handing my half-drunk coffee to Jane, and then Jack held the door open as I grabbed my bag and dashed past him, calling to June, who was at the front desk, to come with us.

'I'm right behind you, Doctor,' she said.

I'm not sure what I was expecting when I reached the scene; perhaps somebody old, sick or out of condition for whom the long flight had been too much. However, there on the floor, under the bright lights of the immigration hall, lay a fine-featured, slim young man, who looked as if he wasn't even thirty years old. I looked back at Jack in surprise and he shrugged, as baffled as I was. When I knelt down next to him he was still conscious but gasping for breath and very frightened.

'I'm Dr Green,' I said. 'Can you tell me what happened?'

I put my hand up as if to loosen the top buttons of his shirt, but his hand shot up as if he were shielding himself from an attacker.

'NO!'

'It's OK, I just want to make it easier for you to breathe,' I said.

'I'm OK, I'm OK,' the man insisted. 'I'm better now.'

He clearly wasn't. 'Do you think you can get up then, if I help you?'

The man nodded but I remained unconvinced. Beads of

sweat gathered around his hairline and above his lip; his eyes panicked.

'What's your name?' I said, offering my arm. 'Is there anybody else travelling with you?'

'No. There's nobody. It's fine.'

He steadied himself, hand on wall, then without another word he took off, almost taking my arm with him, as if tearing to a finishing line.

Stunned, I called out after him, 'Wait! You shouldn't be . . .'

He couldn't have got more than thirty feet, crashing in an unsightly heap just a few seconds into his impromptu sprint.

'Oh my God!' A collective gasp went up in the immigration hall. Everyone looked at the man on the floor and then at me, hot-footing it towards the prone figure, now in even more distress. When I reached him a second time I decided I wasn't taking any nonsense, despite his continued resistance.

'I'm OK.' He was gasping to get his words out.

'Look, you're clearly not OK and I need to check you over,' I said. 'Can you tell me your name, please?'

'It's . . . It's Ali.'

'OK, Ali, I'm just going to take your pulse.'

It was obvious that he was struggling to breathe but a quick check told me he was tachycardic, which means his heart was beating at a faster than normal rate – much faster – and by now he was sweating like a waterfall.

'I think we need to get you into the Health Control Unit, Ali,' I said.

He was still for a moment, dark brown eyes blinking up at me.

'I don't need to,' he said. 'I have to be somewhere.'

'Well, I'm sure it can wait; you're not well,' I said. 'I'll be as quick as I can, I promise.'

With the help of Jack and June, I managed to get him up and the three of us steered him towards HCU, zigzagging through the gaggle of alarmed passengers. Mercifully, the place where he'd collapsed wasn't too far away, so we got him to HCU fairly quickly and without further incident. Once I'd settled him into a cubicle on an examination bed, I encouraged him to loosen his shirt while I asked Megan to call the paramedics, who were always on standby at the port, as I was sure he needed to be taken to hospital.

I pulled Jack to one side to find out if there was anything else he could tell me other than that he'd collapsed in the hall.

'He's from Afghanistan, I think,' he said. 'I noticed him because he's so tall, but I definitely saw him with another man. He was talking to him.'

'But he said he was travelling alone, so where is the other man now?' I said.

'I think he just evaporated into the crowd the second he went down,' Jack said.

I nodded. 'Perhaps you ought to hang around out here, just in case.'

When I turned around, Ali still hadn't undressed and now he was hyperventilating.

'OK, I need to examine you properly.' My voice was stern in the hope he might respond.

It was just the two of us now, but again his hand swept protectively up to his shirt. There was something he didn't want me to see and I was trying not to lose my patience.

'Have you got any chest pain?' I said. His head was moving erratically and I wasn't sure whether he was nodding or shaking it. 'Do you have any medical conditions I should know about? Asthma? Any problems with your chest? Do you take any regular medication?'

Ali just looked up at me; it was as if he wasn't even hearing my voice, yet I knew he could understand me.

'Look, I have to listen to your chest, Ali. I have to find out what's going on.'

His breathing was fast becoming more erratic and, as much as he tried to control it, it was running away with him. Ultimately, self-preservation won the day and he finally released the grip from the front of his shirt and dropped his arm, loosening his buttons to the waist.

Underneath his clothes he was wearing a full-body corset tight and intricate, like a second skin. What a strange thing for a young man to be wearing. It had been pulled in ridiculously tight and must have been really uncomfortable on the flight. Was this the reason he was in the state he was in? Why on earth had he got this thing on? I got stuck in trying to negotiate the fastenings of the thing, but then something weird happened: a flour-like cloud puffed upward, spilling on to my hands. I followed the trail downward to my knees.

'Oh! Goodness!'

I looked up at Ali who sat graveyard still for a second and said nothing. As I continued to feel all my way around the corset, I realized that the seams running downward were, in fact, long compartments with packets of the same white powder sewn into them. The thing was chock-full of what had to be drugs, and it looked like a couple of the compartments had ruptured.

OK, so now what? Discovering huge amounts of drugs on a person wasn't exactly in my remit; that was usually the domain of Customs and the IOs. I had to deal with Ali just like I would any other patient and do what needed to be done medically, as quickly as possible.

'OK, we need to get you out of this,' I said, unfastening the corset as quickly as I could. 'It's preventing you from breathing and we need to get it off.'

By now, Ali had let any thoughts of resistance go. He knew he needed help and I was the only one who was going to give it to him, so he helped get the corset off as best he could while still gasping for air. I finally pulled the thing from around his body, sending another puff of white into the air.

'Ali, what is this?' I said. 'Is it drugs?'

It was a pointless question I already knew the answer to, but for some reason I wanted to give him the option of an explanation before I alerted Customs. Still, he hadn't answered any of my questions so I very much doubted he was going to answer that one.

'OK, I just need to check your legs,' I said and he nodded.

One of his calves was tight and swollen and he winced in pain as I pushed my finger into it.

'I'm sorry, Ali, is that very tender? Did you get up and move around on the flight?'

'No,' he said. 'I didn't get up at all.'

'Well, it looks as if you might have a deep vein thrombosis,' I said. 'We need to get you to hospital because I suspect a bit of a clot has got stuck in your lung.'

My words seemed to spark fresh alarm, so I gave him some oxygen, which seemed to help. Unfortunately, there was nothing else I could do for him at the HCU. The corset had obstructed what we call the venous return, the flow of blood back to the heart from the extremities. That, combined with the fact that he'd been sitting on a long flight, meant that the blood had pooled in his calf veins and then clotted: deep vein thrombosis. Then, as he disembarked from the flight, a classic scenario had unfolded – the calf pump started working again, squeezing the veins in his leg as he started walking, causing a chunk of the clot to break off and travel up to the first place it hit, the lungs. It's called a pulmonary embolism and it occurs when a blood clot travels from the calf through the right side of the heart, lodging in the blood vessels leading to the lung. It was the cause of his collapse, his shortness of breath, sweating and the fact that his heart was going like the clappers.

In severe cases, it can result in sudden death, as had been the case a couple of years earlier when a young bride-to-be collapsed and died a few minutes after disembarking from a flight from Australia. Emma Christoffersen had died from deep vein thrombosis most probably caused by sitting for several hours on the 12,000-mile flight to Heathrow from Sydney. She was a victim of pulmonary embolism, losing consciousness in Arrivals before she collected her luggage, and sadly died on her way to hospital. Since then, there'd been a hell of a lot of publicity on the news and in the press about deep vein thrombosis and pulmonary embolism following long-haul flights, but I'd bet good money that none of them were caused by restrictive corsets full of Class A drugs.

At the hospital Ali would be treated with an anti-coagulant to dissolve the clot, and if they got him there quick enough, my hope was that he'd be OK – at least medically. There was still the not inconsequential matter of his smuggling cocaine or heroin in a strange corset contraption.

'Ali, I'm afraid I'm going to have to let Immigration and also Customs know about this,' I said, gently, indicating the discarded corset.

He managed a nervous smile and nodded, as if he were relieved that it was all finally over. Ali was a drug mule, transporting the drugs for some wealthy dealer, probably for very little money. It was something I was to see a great deal more of as time went on, as well as many similarly ingenious ways for hiding the drugs.

While we waited for the paramedics, I slipped out and told June to alert the Customs Officers about the drugs, and within minutes they were at the door of my office, eager to question Ali.

'Does he need to go straight to hospital, Doctor?' an officer asked me. 'They don't put guards on the door there, you know. It's not a prison. He'll probably do a bunk as soon as he's well again.'

'Well, that may be so, but I'm afraid he does have to go to hospital,' I said, feeling strangely protective towards the young man. 'You've got a couple of minutes to ask him a few questions, but once the ambulance is here he needs to get straight off to Hillingdon A&E.'

Customs were never happy in a situation where a suspected

criminal has to be sent to hospital because it renders them powerless, and that's understandable. They had their job to do just as I did, but I couldn't knowingly put Ali or anyone else's life at risk, criminal or not. As it was, Ali had been lucky we'd got him straight into HCU. If he'd made it out of the airport, he might have been in real trouble.

Jack came back into the room and had a brief word with Ali, relieving him of his passport, while the Customs Officer collected the drugs, which were still puffing out of the corset as he packed it into a clear plastic bag. Within a few minutes, Ali had been scooped up by the paramedics and was gone.

'Well, that was all very . . . I don't know if exciting is the right word,' I said, walking back into the office, where Jane was just finishing up for the night.

'Yes, it did seem a bit heavy,' she said. 'Do you think he's going to be all right?'

'God, I hope so,' I said. 'I mean, I know I'm fairly new at this but all that heroin or whatever it was came as a bit of a shock really, especially sewn into a corset.'

'I can promise you you'll see even stranger the longer you're here,' Jane smiled. 'Was he the first drug mule you've had to deal with?'

'He was, and I have to say he didn't strike me as a drug smuggler,' I said, sitting down.

'It probably wasn't a career choice,' Jane said. 'We see a lot of it, though. People taking all sorts of risks for a tiny amount of money or because they're under threat of harm.'

'Jack said he saw him talking to another man,' I said. 'He probably knew him and ran when he got into trouble.'

'Maybe he was wearing something similar,' Jane said.

She picked up the newspaper we'd been huddled over before Ali's arrival and handed it to me with a smile.

'PUSHOVER,' she announced.

'Who is?'

'Fifteen across,' she said. 'Drink's knocked back, linger for piece of cake. Pushover.'

'Oh! Really? God, I'm never going to get the hang of this,' I said.

'The job or the *Telegraph* cryptic?' Jane said, raising an eyebrow. 'You're doing great, Steph, and I'm sure you'll get used to both.'

Maybe, I thought, but if tonight was anything to go by it was going to take time. Still, I'd taken this job because I wanted a challenge, hadn't I? Something different. And from the look of things that's exactly what I'd got.

The following morning I contacted Hillingdon to check on Ali's condition. Following up on patients was something I'd naturally do less of the longer I worked at HCU, as it was impossible to keep track with so many new cases appearing but back then I was still keen to know the outcome of a case.

The team at Hillingdon A&E had done the usual investigations, which had confirmed the diagnosis of pulmonary embolism. The good news was that he'd got to hospital in time for the outcome to be a positive one, and now was in recovery. He'd probably spend about a week in hospital. Jack told me that he'd actually had over 5kg of heroin wrapped around him, a stash he'd been transporting for some faceless drug dealer back in Afghanistan. Ali may have been the first drug mule I came across at Heathrow and the circumstances had surprised me, but he wasn't the last or even the only one in a drug-filled undergarment. There were many similar discoveries to come.

# 7

# the mule train

BEFORE LONG I'D SETTLED INTO THE JOB, and was used to the run-of-the-mill medical activity at Heathrow: from standard X-rays to looking over drugs and medicines coming into the country, or running health checks on asylum seekers. Many days followed a similar routine, but these were punctuated with moments of high drama and, for the first few years of my time at Heathrow, a lot of those moments came with the afternoon Air Jamaica flight from Kingston. The flight came in at about 3pm and Immigration would regularly interview people and then siphon them off for further questioning, filtering them through to a holding room before they ended up with me in HCU, mainly for X-rays to check for TB.

At around 4.30 one Friday afternoon, an IO called David bounded into HCU with news of that day's Air Jamaica flight, just as I finished strapping up an elderly man who'd fallen over his suitcase in the immigration hall and cut his arm quite badly.

'We've got quite a few detainees in the holding room awaiting X-rays,' he said. 'It's getting pretty backed up in there.'

David was one of the jollier IOs. A large man of about forty, he delivered news, however serious or sombre, with a cheesy grin that generally left people hanging for a punch line, and this occasion, around six months into my job, was no exception.

'The Kingston flight's always a busy one,' he grinned. 'We've detained a group of four single young men coming through Immigration. Could you check them over please, Doctor? And we'll need to get them X-rayed.'

'Four? Why were so many detained?' I asked.

'All a bit vague as to why they're here,' David said. 'And it was a case of the good old "Auntie" story with a couple of them.'

I knew what he meant straight away. A fair few of the young Jamaican men who had been detained during my time at Heathrow seemed to have the same reason for being here; they were coming to the UK to visit their auntie for a few days. It had become a bit of a running joke among anyone working in and around Border Control, because many of the auntie-visiting detainees turned out to be the ones who had something to hide. Of course, that didn't mean this was the case with the men who were currently sitting glumly in HCU waiting for me to send them for an X-ray, but it always seemed odd that none of the men coming to visit auntie could ever tell you her name, nor could they pinpoint a postcode, let alone an address, of where she might reside. Also, auntie never came to meet them at the airport. Ever. It was this kind of vague and dubious story that would often set alarm bells ringing with David and the rest of the IOs, and that's when a person might be detained and questioned further about the purpose of their visit. Meanwhile, we at HCU had to X-ray them, as we did all detainees, just in case they were carrying any nasty infections, particularly TB.

While three of the men waited to be checked over, I headed to where Jane had just finished performing an X-ray on the fourth, but what should have been a straightforward check for TB fast turned into something else entirely.

'Let's have a look, shall we?' I said. Jane looked up and then turned the screen towards me.

I knew from the expression on Jane's face that something was up, and she was right. There was something showing on the X-ray that undoubtedly shouldn't have been there.

Lungs extend down the body much further than you might imagine, particularly behind the liver, and when taking a chest X-ray it's important to make sure that the whole of the lung fields, from top to bottom, are in the film. So the image also tends to include the top of the stomach and the transverse colon. Bowel stasis during a flight means that there is often more air in the bowel than normal (hence serious farting when you disembark and everything gets moving again), and so in an X-ray solid objects in the stomach or colon can show up against the collected air.

'What does that look like to you?' Jane said, as I peered at the image.

I could make out what looked like a series of perfectly even, inch-long ovals, neatly lined up in the bubble at the top of the man's stomach. If this were food or faeces lurking, the surface would have been uneven, but the shapes sitting at the top of this guy's stomach were too smooth to be either.

'Whatever it is, there seems to be a lot of it,' I said.

Jane shook her head. 'I've come across this on X-rays a few times lately: packages full of drugs, probably cocaine. I think we're looking at the inside of a man who has swallowed a whole lot of it. All wrapped up in condoms.'

This was the first time I'd encountered anything like this, but the facts were staggering. People smuggling drugs into the UK have been known to swallow up to 200 packets of cocaine using this method, and in most cases they're doing it for somebody else, either because they are desperate for money or are doing it against their will. Swallowing cocaine in this way is a dangerous and precise undertaking that has to be rehearsed thoroughly. Later that day, one of the longer-serving HCOs explained to me how it worked. Potential carriers have to practise the swallowing part of the operation beforehand, but instead of filled condoms they use large pieces of carrot, which didn't make sense to me at all. I mean, how was swallowing one of your five-a-day going to set you up for wolfing down a couple of hundred prophylactics chock-full of Bolivian marching powder? It would have been like petting a cat in preparation for taming a lion.

Once the candidate was ready for the main event – swallowing the drugs for real – they take loperamide or something similar, which slows down the motility of the gut. It's what you might take to stop diarrhoea, but in this case it ensures that they don't pass any of the drug-filled condoms mid-flight. After they've bunged themselves up and swallowed the drugs they can head to the airport and board the plane. Once they're en route, the rule is that they mustn't eat much or move around the plane in case it stimulates bowel movement.

It's incredibly dangerous, of course, but what makes it even more of a tragedy is that most of them are paid as little as $200 to risk life as well as liberty. I'm aware that's probably a fortune to someone living in poverty in Kingston, but it still shocks me that somebody would risk everything for such a small amount. Of course, those desperate to get drugs into

Europe clearly know exactly who to target for these hazardous jobs – poor or disadvantaged young men and women who need the money, or people whose families are threatened and so have no choice.

Understandably, many of the carriers were totally 'wired' when they got off the plane – sometimes because there had been some kind of cocaine leakage into their system, sometimes because they were just so terrified, or perhaps both. This was often why they were so easily identifiable coming through Immigration. As well as that, a young single man flying halfway around the globe to spend time with an auntie he barely knows is hardly the most plausible story in the world, is it?

When I walked into the examination room, the young man with the packages in his stomach was perched on the end of the examination bed – seriously on edge. And why wouldn't you be, with a stomach full of cocaine? I asked his name and he looked up at me, silent and furrow-browed.

'Do you mind telling me your name?' I asked again.

Grudgingly, he told me it was Richard.

'Richard, I'm Dr Green,' I said. 'I just need to have a quick look at you, if that's OK.'

I'd have to go carefully from here on in. I was walking a fine line between getting the job done as quickly and efficiently as I could, and trying to keep the guy from freaking out. And I had to do it all without letting him know what was happening and that we were on to him. Still, I'd been fairly well briefed on how to deal with a situation like this, hadn't I? Protocol was that we never told a detainee if we'd found anything dodgy. We were doctors simply checking for any infections, just to be safe. A few of them believed what we told them, but most got decidedly jumpy so I spoke softly to him, reassuring him as I worked.

'I'm just checking your lungs and your breathing. Making sure everything's working as it should be.'

'OK,' he muttered.

He wasn't convinced; that much was obvious. And was it me or did this guy have a particularly mean-looking face? I'd seen the other three guys in the holding room and they looked quite affable and relatively angelic next to this guy. Why couldn't I have got one of them to examine first?

It was clear that Richard was pretty wired: eyes darting around the room, body tense, sweating. Was that simply due to nerves or had there been a leakage of the drug into his system? God forbid it was that. A massive hit of coke at this point might send his fear and paranoia levels through the roof and I could be at serious risk. The last thing I or any of us at the unit needed was a terrified, strong, young guy, high on Class As, kicking off all of a sudden – particularly as we were an all-women unit. All our HCOs had to be women because the job regularly involved the undressing and X-raying of young girls and women, some from Muslim countries, and it was more culturally acceptable for this to be done by a woman. It's one of the few jobs where the gender of the applicant may be specified and it is exempt from the Sex Discrimination Act.

'OK, I'm all finished,' I said, removing my stethoscope.

'Am I sick?' he said.

'No. I don't think you are,' I said.

'Then I can go?'

'Not up to me, I'm afraid.'

'Why? Why are you keeping me here if I'm not sick?' he said.

'I . . . I mean . . . we have to wait for Immigration to give you the all clear before we can . . . I just need to make a quick call, Richard,' I said. 'Can you give me a minute?'

Soon after, David and another IO came in to escort Richard back to Immigration. I took David to one side as the other officer led Richard out of the examination room.

'He's carrying drugs in his stomach and there's a lot of it,' I said.

David nodded like he'd been expecting this news. 'OK, I'll let Customs know.'

'Look, he's very on edge and needs to be kept calm until he passes the packages,' I said. 'If any of that stuff gets into his system it could kill him. Could you call the paramedics if you're at all concerned about him?'

'Got it. We'll do our best,' David said.

I imagined that would probably be the last I saw of Richard. As a smuggler, he'd be confined to one of the cells at Heathrow while officers waited for nature to take its course and the packages to pass through his system.

A while later, Jane came into my office with news of Richard's fate.

'Apparently he's still in the holding room,' she said as we sat down together. 'David told me that there aren't any cells so they're waiting for one to free up.'

'God, are Customs that full up today?' I said.

'The X-ray machine has been pretty much flat out,' she said. 'Maybe they'll have to send him over to Harmondsworth Detention Centre. There are still two guys in the holding room who haven't even been X-rayed yet.'

It was true. Sometimes, like a table at the hippest new restaurant or top price seats for an Adele concert, cells were hard to come by and there might be a long wait. Once a cell did finally free up, Customs Officers would confine Richard and wait until he excreted the large stashes in his bowels so they could retrieve them. (If their job has any perks, I'm pretty sure this isn't one of them.) They're able to do this because the cells at Heathrow have a special, enclosed toilet system, which is self-contained so the evidence can't be flushed away. That being said, it wasn't always the speediest of processes. Sometimes, due to the amount of the loperamide a carrier had taken, it took a long time for the drugs to pass through the body and come out the other end, and at this point our man wasn't showing any signs of wanting to unload his contraband. The obvious solution would be to administer some sort of laxative to help things along, but I was unable to do that in case it caused one of the condoms to perforate or even burst, sending massive amounts of cocaine into his bloodstream and surely killing him. From what I'd been told, it wouldn't be the first time it had happened. We just had to wait, and sometimes the wait was long. One legendary detainee went something like thirty days before passing the drugs. Can you imagine thirty days without going to the loo? I have to say I suspect the story is apocryphal.

One afternoon, a few months after the experience with Richard, a distraught young Jamaican woman was brought into HCU to be examined and X-rayed.

Whenever I showed a woman into a cubicle, I'd give her the requisite cotton gown and do a sort of mime, demonstrating the correct way to put it on – then I'd leave her to get on with it. We always had passengers undress before the X-ray so that no metal zips, bra clasps and so on obscured the image.

One thing that struck me particularly when people (especially women) were asked to undress was how their reactions to being examined differed, depending on where they had come from. The Ghanaians, for example, would invariably be standing there completely stripped when I walked back into the cubicle five minutes later. Breasts out, no gown, no inhibitions. They had no shame in their naked body. In contrast, the Pakistani or Bengali women were the absolute opposite. They would often simply put the gown on over their clothes, so I'd have to show them what I wanted them to do again and then hold up the gown so they could hide behind it, before helping them into it while also averting my eyes to respect their privacy and dignity. They were always so shy – the process was quite an ordeal for them.

As well as that, we saw the Indian girls who had come over to get married, often adorned in extraordinarily intricate jewellery. While undressing, they meticulously laid it out on the benches in each cubicle. The jewellery was clearly very precious, as the young women wanted to make a good impression with their new families. It was fascinating just watching and helping them undo their saris, which are like a complex work of art. There seemed to be hundreds of safety pins, holding it in perfect position around the chest and then over and under. I thought them exquisite. On most occasions, I'd end up physically helping them undress because they didn't speak a word of English, and it was just easier to do it rather than explain it.

The Somali women would undress to reveal incredible henna tattoos on their hands and arms – quite stunning – and they all wore patchouli oil. One could always recognize the Somalis by this strong, sweet and heady perfume; it hit you the moment you walked into the room.

These brief moments with our passengers were a part of my job that I loved: all the different cultures and their varying attitudes passing through under my gaze. I found it fascinating that a woman's upbringing and her culture could be so apparent in just that little thing – undressing and putting on a simple cotton gown.

On this occasion when I walked back into the examination cubicle, the young woman was already dressed in one of the plain cotton gowns. The simplicity of the gown made her look innocent, almost childlike, although she was probably in her early twenties.

'Hello, I'm Dr Green. What's your name?'

'Anya,' she said, shifting on the bed. 'And none of this was my choice.'

'What wasn't your choice, Anya?' I said.

Her head went down and she closed her eyes. 'The drugs. It wasn't my choice to bring the drugs.'

It was hard to imagine the desperation that led some people

to undertake a perilous task like carrying drugs inside them, and looking at this seemingly innocent and frightened young woman it was almost impossible. It had been her erratic, nervy behaviour that had alerted Customs. Anya had been looking around like a scared rabbit and sweating – a mess, the attending IO had said.

'So you are carrying drugs inside you?' I asked. 'You swallowed them?'

'I think you already know this,' she said. 'Cocaine.'

It was very unusual for somebody to offer this information voluntarily, but this young woman was clearly quite bright. Perhaps she knew very well what an X-ray could show up.

'OK, well it's better that you've told me,' I said. 'It makes things a lot easier. I'll still need to examine you and get you X-rayed though. Is that OK, Anya?'

'I suppose it is.'

I rarely got into detailed conversations with detainees about the whys and wherefores of what they were doing, but on this occasion I felt compelled to ask her why she would do something so perilous: something that could see her locked up or, worse still, dead.

'I told you, it wasn't my choice,' she said. 'I was made to do it.'

'By who? Who would make a young girl like you do such a dangerous thing?'

103

'He's a man my brother knows,' she said. 'He's a well-known man in the area where we live. A drug dealer with a big business. He's not a good person. People are afraid of him.'

'So what happened? Did he threaten you?' I asked.

'Not me!' Anya was trembling. 'My family. He and his business partners came to our home and showed me a gun. He said he would use it on my mother and children if I did not agree to bring the drugs for him. I could not take the risk so . . . I was recruited.'

Her tears told me she was telling the truth, but it was hard to hear.

'I have two children, a boy and a girl,' she said. 'Of course I love them and I can't stand the thought of them being harmed. I just want to get home to them but now I've been caught I just don't know . . .' Her voice tailed off and her face twisted in pain. This woman had been willing to do anything to protect her kids, as most mothers would, but then this was such a far cry from my own safe life, it seemed impossible to even contemplate.

'They took me to a house where they made me prepare for the task. They told me it was hard but that I could do it. I had to practise with food until was I ready to do the job.'

I looked into Anya's eyes, trying just for a second to put myself in her place. Of course, I'd have done what she did and swallowed the drugs. What choice would I have had? In

Jamaica she probably wouldn't have had the resources to be able to fight against the drug dealers, nor the faith that if she'd told law enforcement what was happening that they'd be able to protect her. The gangs seemed to wield so much power there and there was no one she could have gone to for help. It was clear that if there'd been any other way out of this, she'd have taken it. There wasn't. So she'd boarded a plane for England with a stomach full of these condoms – each one of which contained enough cocaine to stop her heart instantly if it burst.

'Anya, you have to tell the officers what you just told me,' I said. 'You have to let them know that you were forced into this.'

She nodded. 'I will. I just have to pray that this man doesn't harm my family once he knows I failed.'

'I'm sure that won't happen,' I said, but how could I possibly be sure?

Tears fell again.

'I just want to get home to my children,' she said.

'Well, I'm going to make sure that you're looked after while you're here,' I said. 'You'll be closely monitored while the drugs pass through your system so nothing bad is going to happen, OK?'

Anya wiped her eyes, nodding slowly. It was a heartbreaking thing to have to watch. This young woman had simply been trying to protect her family, her children, but now she might well end up in prison for two years in the UK before being sent back to Jamaica. The brutality of it all was very hard to come to terms with, but at least Anya would come out of it alive.

Just a week later, I boarded a flight to record the death of a young woman who'd been taken ill on the way from Kingston to London, mid-flight. She'd indicated to a stewardess that she was unwell, and as the flight went on she became sweaty and anxious, complaining that her heart was thumping. In desperation, she'd eventually confided to the stewardess that she had drugs in her stomach and that she needed help, but by then there was very little anyone could do. One or more of the packages had burst and was seeping into her system, and that amount of cocaine in the bloodstream is catastrophic. She never made it across the Atlantic. Her heart just stopped.

Of course it angered me, knowing that all these drugs were coming into the country. Working in psychiatry, I'd seen first hand how they screwed up lives: patients with psychosis brought on by heavy or extended drug use, or those who were self-medicating because of the symptoms they had, or who'd overdosed. Yes, some people can use drugs recreationally without any ill effects, but as we all know that's not universal – and it's not just the Class As. I admitted lots of people with no prior mental health conditions to psychiatric units – young men mostly – suffering from a drug-induced psychosis. Some of it was caused by cocaine or amphetamine use, but also marijuana, which people often think of as harmless or benign. This is true for some people; for others it's anything but.

I admitted one young Scottish man of about twenty-one who'd out of the blue accused his father of sexual abuse. Of course, a claim like this has to be taken seriously, but the details that he gave us were very far-fetched, and the accusations he was making against various people turned out to be a delusional belief caused by psychosis brought on by cannabis use. The tragedy of this case was that he never got better. He was a delightful young man who came from a loving family who were devastated by the whole thing. It wasn't even massive overuse of the drug, but it was too much for him. We tried various medications, but his delusional beliefs remained and we just couldn't make him better.

Eventually, a joint programme was set up between Heathrow and Kingston airports with some of our Customs Officers seconded over there with state-of-the art-scanners in an attempt to stop the drug mules getting on to flights in the first place. No doubt after that the dealers started looking for alternative routes. Sadly there were always going to be drug mules pushed through somewhere, risking their lives to peddle someone else's wares.

I always felt incredibly sad seeing the men and women who were detained for carrying. They never had the look of people who were particularly prosperous. It certainly wasn't these unfortunate drug mules at whose feet I laid the blame. They were just victims of the drug lords and cartels that had forced them into this life. Pawns in the big, fast-moving machine of somebody else's drug empire. Like Richard, Anya and the young girl who'd died on the plane, these were the people taking all the risk for none of the gain.

# 8

# stowaways

ONE OF THE BEST THINGS about my job was that I didn't have to take it home with me – at least not most of the time. In 2002 Chris and I moved to a farmhouse called Little Newbury. It belonged to his grandmother, who'd recently gone into sheltered accommodation. Little Newbury was an arable farm, growing wheat, linseed and other crops. A local man farmed it for us, and it also had some paddocks and stables rented to local horse owners. It had been in Chris's family for years, and his father and uncle had been born right there in the farmhouse. We ended up staying there for eleven happy years, right through my time at Heathrow, and I found that the job, though high-pressured and stressful at times, had much more equilibrium with my home life than the brutal hours of a hospital doctor.

A lot of this new balance was because I rarely worried out-of-hours about my patients; my relationship with them was so transient. Yes, it might be intense at the time of consultation, but once they were gone, they were gone. My thoughts might have lingered over something or someone I had seen during the course of a working day, but there were no plans to be made, no follow-up to think about. It was that ongoing responsibility that had taken its toll on me working in psychiatry. At Port Health, once I had passed my patients on to other authorities, it was out of my hands.

As I said, this was *most* of the time. But there were a few moments that lingered for longer that I would have liked – shocking or sometimes incredibly moving episodes that came out of the blue or were impossible to shake from my mind and leave behind at the airport exit. One such episode was the tragic death of two stowaways, who were little more than children.

It's ironic; I'd told myself that night was going to be a quiet one. A night during which my most taxing undertaking was to be the unwrapping of an egg and cress on multigrain and perhaps the turning of a few pages of the novel I'd started three months ago but hardly made a dent in. As it turned out, I was too tired for either. By midnight, I was tucked up under my scratchy blankets, earplugs in to block out the not-too-distant sound of hammering and building repairs being done mostly at night when the airport was quiet. I was all ready for sleep.

As I languished in that sublime feathery state, somewhere between consciousness and sleep – the phone. Of course, the phone. My body on autopilot, I picked up. Years of working as a doctor develops an array of skills, one of which is the ability to sit up in bed and get some way into a conversation before fully waking up. This was one of those times.

'Dr Green speaking.'

I was hoping for something inconsequential: clarification on a case from earlier in the day, a quick question or inquiry. Something that I could deal with, you know, horizontally.

The male caller spoke flatly. 'We've found two stowaways on a flight from Ghana.'

Oh, so not inconsequential then. 'Wow, do you know how they got on board the flight?'

'They didn't get on it, I'm afraid,' the man said. 'The boys hid in the undercarriage of the plane. And they're both dead.'

Now I was awake.

'In the undercarriage?' I said. 'How?'

'I know. It sounds unlikely but that's what's happened,' he said. 'Can you come down to stand number 4, Terminal 3 to record a death?'

'Yes of course. I'll be right down.'

I felt a little bit sick as I headed to the stand. I was used to attending deaths on flights – it's part of what I did, and although never pleasant, I was used to it. In the majority of cases I was able to make my peace with it and move on. This felt different, though. Boys he'd said, hadn't he? Not men, *boys*. And stowing away in the undercarriage of a plane; I struggled to imagine how that might even have been possible. My mind was racing as I reached the stand, grasping at thoughts of what might have finished off these two poor lads. Had they suffocated? Frozen to death? Been crushed?

I was greeted by a small band of solemn-faced security guards and ground crew, unusually quiet. My eyes darted around for blanket-covered bodies somewhere in the vicinity, but there were none.

'Have you removed them?' I asked.

One of the ground crew shook his head. 'They're still in there. Can you certify the deaths before we remove them?'

I wasn't sure I could, but the crewman and I made our way towards the Ghana Airways DC-10 airliner anyway.

'After the plane landed, the ground crew went to secure the chocks in front of the wheels and they saw a hand fall out of one of the wheel bays,' he said.

By now I could see the dangling hand for myself. A shudder ran up my back.

'How do you think they got in there without anyone seeing them?' I asked. 'God, it's impossible to even get near a plane at Heathrow.'

'You know, there was a film recently where someone pulled a

stunt like this,' the crewman said. 'A bloke got into the wheels of a plane and he survived. Maybe these guys were copying that. Like a prank.'

'Some prank,' I said, looking upward. 'Look, I think it's going to be too difficult for me to do this with them in situ. Its dark and cramped and I . . .' The officer was hanging on my every word. 'I think it'd be better if you brought the bodies down.'

'If that's what you think,' he said.

Getting the bodies out wasn't easy but there didn't seem to be any trauma or damage to them. They certainly weren't crushed as I suspected they might be, so there had obviously been enough room for them to climb comfortably into the wheel bay. It seemed so implausible that anyone would under-take something so dangerous, even in desperation. Closer examination of the boys made things a little clearer and my heart sank as I looked down at them. These boys were young. Barely even teenagers. To me, this didn't feel like some des-perate attempt to escape Ghana. Maybe the air crewman was right. Maybe it had been just a childish prank. The thought of it made the situation feel even uglier.

This wasn't the first time something like this had happened. In 1999, two young African stowaways were also found in the landing gear of a plane, this time in Brussels. Koita and Tounkara, fifteen and sixteen respectively, were found dead while the plane was being refuelled. One of the boys had been carrying a handwritten letter explaining that although they knew the dangers of their plan, the struggles of life in Guinea, West Africa, had driven them to it. The letter was written in shaky French and addressed to the 'Excellencies, gentlemen-members and those responsible in Europe', saying, 'If you see that we have sacrificed ourselves and lost our lives, it is because we suffer too much in Africa and need your help to struggle against poverty and war. Please excuse us very much for daring to write this letter.'

Here at Heathrow, neither of the boys was carrying anything of note with them. One had an empty wallet, while the other was carrying a broken padlock. It was clear they had no idea of the freezing temperatures they were going to face up there (their clothes were suitable for the heat of Africa, with one of the boys wearing open-toed sandals). The plane had just completed a six-hour journey from Accra, cruising at an oxygen-starved altitude of 38,000 feet in temperatures that could have plunged to minus 50 or 60 degrees Fahrenheit. I assumed the boys had died from a combination of hypothermia and hypoxia, that is extreme cold and a lack of oxygen, and that's what the coroner's report confirmed. What was even more unbelievable was that the boys had managed to stow away on the plane in broad daylight – the flight from Accra had been a daytime one, and only a few days after an attack on Mombasa airport in Kenya; security at African airports was expected to have been tightened. Clearly it hadn't been.

I had to think long and hard to remember exactly what had happened, to the point that I even asked Chris if it really was just me who attended the death of these boys and to help me with all the details.

'Yes, I remember you phoning me the minute you'd done it,' he assured me. 'I remember it very well. You were the only doctor there, Steph.'

A good friend of mine suggested that I might have been blanking it out all these years because I'd found it so distressing. Maybe that's true, I don't know, but I really had to dig deep and do my research to remember what happened. In fact, while we were exploring the facts of the story together, hoping to find any more details of why the boys might have done such a thing, Chris unearthed more sad tales. One was of two young brothers, who'd tried to stow away in the wheel of a flight from Delhi. Miraculously, one of them survived, but the younger of the two, just nineteen, fell from the plane over London after freezing to death. More recently, in 2013, a young man was found on a pavement in west London, having stowed away in the landing gear of a British Airways flight from Angola. His body had fallen from the plane as its undercarriage opened for its descent into Heathrow. He was found with a single pound coin in his pocket, trying to get to

London to make a new life for himself. Instead he had died thousands of feet up in the sky.

When I look back at it now, I think of it as more shocking than distressing. It was so out of the ordinary it almost didn't seem real and was hard for all of us to get our heads around. By then, after four years as a doctor, I'd recorded enough deaths to know that the only way to process it was to push those thoughts aside and do my job because if I really had stopped to think about every death, especially ones like this, my work life would be too heartbreaking. My sole part in this was to confirm that the two Ghanaians had died and to record the time of death. Even then it was hard not to think of their poor mothers and fathers. How were they ever going to be able to come to terms with how their children had died? It was such a waste.

I headed back to the unit where Megan was sipping a cappuccino and reading the paper.

'You look terrible,' she said. 'I'm not surprised, though.'

'You've heard about the boys then?'

She nodded. 'I have to say I'm glad I didn't have to attend, Stephanie. Do you really think it could have been a prank? I can't really get my head around it.'

'It might have been; they were very young,' I told her. 'Too young. Just young kids in T-shirts and sandals.'

Perhaps if it had happened a few months before, the boys'

deaths might not have shaken me as much, but Chris and I were married by now and had been planning to start a family, so motherhood and children were very much in the forefront of my mind. We were in a new home and it felt like the right time. In fact, it wasn't long after this affecting incident that I discovered I was pregnant with our first child, Henry, and that was when Chris and I were thrown into a very different kind of drama.

I don't remember what night of the week it was now, but I do remember that I was suffering from the nagging nausea and exhaustion of early pregnancy, to the point where I'd taken myself off to bed by nine, and Chris wasn't far behind. I was the one who was dog-tired, but it was Chris who was dead to the world about ten seconds after his head hit the pillow, while I tossed and turned. Don't you hate it when that happens? Where was the fairness in that? God, I was due at work the next day, a twenty-four-hour shift no less, but the way I felt I wasn't sure I was going to make it. If only that had been all I had to worry about that night.

At about one in the morning the phone rang. Or did it? It was one of those times where I could hear the sound of a phone but wasn't sure if it was real or if I was dreaming it. I half opened my eyes and saw that Chris hadn't moved – so I ignored it too. But it kept going . . . and going . . . so in the end Chris sat up and answered it, his voice a froggy croak.

'Hello . . . Yes, I . . . what? You're kidding . . . Shit!'

That was enough to make me open my eyes and sit up too. 'Chris?' He was already up and getting dressed and my heart was banging in my chest. 'What is it?'

'The fucking pub's on fire,' he said. 'That was one of the live-in staff. Apparently, there are five fire crews there already.'

'Five? Jesus Christ!'

Within minutes, we were in the car careering through the night towards the Trout, doing our best to keep calm and safe on the dark roads. There were several staff who lived at the pub and it had six guest rooms, some of which were occupied. A huge fire taking hold was unthinkable. As we came over the long hill leading down to the pub, Chris took in a panicky breath.

'Oh my God, look at it, Steph!'

I couldn't speak. I could see the flames leaping out of the roof – it looked as if they were a mile high. A knot twisted in my stomach; I felt so awful for Chris. Just a week or so before, he and his business partner had put the finishing touches to a beautiful new dining room and the six smart guest bedrooms. On top of that, Paddy Burt, the well-known hotel reviewer for the *Telegraph*, had just given the Trout an absolutely glowing review in the Saturday paper, and now it was on fire. This was devastating. When we reached the pub, we jumped out of the car, fast realizing that there was nothing we could do; we just stood there and watched as a big part of our livelihood went up in flames in front of our eyes.

The local fire crews eventually managed to put the fire out, aided by the fact that the pub is right by a river. Chris stood next to me looking drained and dazed throughout, as we both wondered what on earth might have caused such a blaze.

I can't even remember what time we got to bed, but I felt even more sick the next morning, and I just couldn't face going to work. I couldn't cite morning sickness as the reason for my absence – I didn't want to tell anyone at work about the pregnancy until I had passed the twelve-week point – so I just called Dr Thana and told him about the pub. Of course he was very sympathetic about it and told me to take all the time that I needed, and that Dr Sood would cover me that day.

It transpired that someone had dropped a smouldering cigarette on a sofa. Just that tiny moment of carelessness had been the cause of all this. The good news was that everyone who'd been resident in the pub had escaped unhurt, but several of the bedrooms were badly damaged, as was Chris's shiny new dining room.

Still, a small miracle happened as the sun came up. With Chris's dad being a local man – his family has lived in that region for generations – many of the local tradesmen as well as good friends rallied round us. Tarpaulins were hoisted up, major damage was patched up until it could be redecorated properly, and, somewhat amazingly, the Trout opened that very night. Chris and I could hardly believe it. OK, so everything was a little 'take us as you find us', there was no food aside from a few bags of Kettle Chips, and more than a faint whiff of smoke, but the bar was open and serving pints. Everyone had this determination to keep it going, and we did.

Chris's brother-in-law is in marketing, so the following day he put out a press release about the fire, sending it to the *Telegraph* which had waxed lyrical about the pub just a week or so before. The paper printed an article in their next edition. The headline was . . . 'Pub on fire after hot review!'

# 9

# precious parcels

ASIDE FROM THE ODD BOUT of grisly morning sickness, I enjoyed being pregnant, and work chugged along much the same as it always had. The bonus was that once they knew I was pregnant, all the HCOs fussed around me like mad, making sure I rested and didn't exhaust myself, and I worked right up until eight months.

I don't know if it was the fact that I was about to have one myself, but babies and pregnancy seemed to be a real feature at work during that period. For a kick-off, there seemed to be an abundance of women coming into the UK, hoping to have their babies here – the NHS being a fairly big draw as far as giving birth goes. Immigration often brought in pregnant women who they suspected might just be coming to the UK to have their babies because they believed the care was better.

They were right: the resources, the aftercare, and the fact that it's free at the point of use. Despite the fact that the NHS is constantly struggling, it's pretty much the gold standard as far as healthcare goes. As good as anywhere else in the world, give or take a couple of European countries. Most of these women appeared to be on the wealthier side and the worry was they wanted to take advantage of a better health service than the one they had in their own country – for free. It was an ongoing issue. There was a recent case in the press about a Nigerian woman who came over to the UK and had twins by C-section. After her children were born, the twin babies had problems to the extent that their lives were in danger so, of course, the hospital did everything it could to treat them and look after them. Unfortunately, the twins ended up being in hospital for an extended period, costing hundreds of thousands of pounds to the UK taxpayer, and with the Nigerian government refusing to look after them or indeed foot the bill, it can be quite a sticky issue for Immigration.

My main task when a woman was coming into the country pregnant was to determine gestation and whether it might be twins – the latter can be quite tricky – while Immigration made sure she had return tickets and resources to fund her stay in the UK. For some women it can be quite dangerous to fly in the third trimester, after week twenty-seven; in fact some airlines won't carry women over thirty weeks pregnant without a letter from a GP or obstetrician. That certainly didn't deter some of these women, many of whom told me they'd just come over to London to buy baby clothes. A woman with money might also be able to obtain fake obstetrician letters giving false information about her gestation and whether or not she was fit to fly. Somebody might hand me a letter saying they were fourteen weeks pregnant and I could clearly see they were closer to twenty-four. I even saw false ultrasound reports, with dates on but no name. On more than one occasion I had a woman show me scans saying things like, 'Look, I was four months pregnant three days ago.' But there's no name on the scan and she looks ready to give birth at any moment.

It wasn't unusual for the IOs to bring women to HCU – particularly from certain countries where Immigration believed the practice to be prevalent at the time – for me to check them over. One day Jack did so. The woman looked more than a little confused about why she might be in my office. A statuesque and, shall we say, well-built woman, she was in a beautiful, traditional dress with a colourful turban and flowing robes. Her pleasant face looked stricken with concern as Jack sat her down and asked me if I would be kind enough to check her over.

'For what?' I asked.

'I think she might be pregnant,' he said.

After Jack left, I set about examining the woman, but I had an inkling about this one and felt more than a little awkward feeling around her tummy, especially with the strange look she was giving me. Still, she was silent and affable throughout so I just got on with it. I could usually tell just by looking at a woman whether she was pregnant or just on the large side, and, as it turned out, this woman fell into the latter category.

When I'd finished the examination, she smiled at me knowingly and I escorted her back outside again.

'She's not pregnant, she's just a bit overweight,' I told Jack, surreptitiously. 'She's OK to go through.'

During my first pregnancy I had to attend one of the saddest cases during my time at Heathrow, the death of a baby en route to the UK. Matilde was a little girl on her way to receive what might have been life-saving treatment. Travelling from Portugal, she was due to undergo specialist therapy, but the poor mite never made it, and I was called to record her death.

At Heathrow, there are priests, rabbis, humanists and religious folk of all faiths and denominations on hand, so once I'd taken down all the available information on the case, I asked June to call Father Donovan, a Roman Catholic priest, and ask him to accompany me on board. There he could maybe say a prayer, be of some comfort to the family while I recorded the death, hopefully making the moment a little less clinical than it might have been had I gone alone.

The flight had already been disembarked when Father Donovan and I reached the stand. On this occasion, there was no need to hold up the rest of the passengers, as this wasn't a death caused by any kind of infection. As we headed along the walkway towards the door of the aircraft, I was steeling myself to face distraught, perhaps even hysterical, parents – and who could blame them? Their child had been sick ever since she was born with severe medical problems. This pilgrimage to the UK was something for them to hold on to. A chance, at least, that their daughter might be saved. I thought about how full of hope they must have been when they boarded the plane in Lisbon, just a couple of hours before. Yes, they must have faced the possibility of losing Matilde a hundred times, but there was a sad irony in the fact that they'd almost got here. Tragically, in the end, the journey had proved too much for her.

Despite all this, when I stepped aboard the plane, Father Donovan two steps behind me, I was met with a scene of hushed serenity that took my breath away. The cabin lights were dimmed and everything was so calm and quiet; it was hard to imagine that such a tragedy had just taken place. Right at the back of the plane, Matilde's mother was cuddling her while her father looked down at her, stroking her face. As I got closer, the man looked up at me but the woman didn't take her eyes off her daughter for a second.

'She looks so peaceful,' I said, gently.

'She is now,' the woman said.

Matilde was no more than a year old, and as I moved closer, the sight of her puffy skin and the little feeding tube in her nose belied the vision of a healthy little girl. At their side were a couple of cabin crew who were clearly taking the most wonderful care of them. It was an uncomplicated, almost beautiful scene: a mother cradling her precious daughter, as if she were sleeping. Eventually, the woman looked up at me, her eyes wet, and I smiled back reassuringly because that was all I could do. She'd done her very best – all she could have done – and even now after she was gone, her quiet dignity in the face of such sadness was quite remarkable.

I went to bed that night feeling the sorrow of those parents. By then, they would no longer even be holding their baby, who would be lying in a mortuary somewhere overnight before they could take her back home. I'd met those parents, they were more than just faces to me, and so I felt quite devastated. The death of a child is always hard, but this one was particularly poignant for me as a new mother-to-be.

In contrast, babies occasionally brought moments of great joy in HCU, and being relatively rare these too remained with me. One such moment came as I was about to go on maternity leave, in the shape of a brand-new family. Lola and Joe were a lovely English couple who, on paper, seemed to have a great life. Both were solicitors who'd set up their own small but successful conveyancing practice, they were reasonably well off, had a nice house in Kent and went on far-flung holidays to exotic places. I don't often find out all that much about my patients for the short time I see them in HCU but Lola liked to talk, barely stopping for breath from the minute she walked into the treatment room with her husband who was carrying their beautiful new baby girl.

'I couldn't get pregnant,' she told me. 'IVF just wouldn't work for me. Joe wanted to find a surrogate at first, didn't you, Joe?'

Joe opened his mouth to speak but wasn't quick enough.

'It got to the stage when it was all I could think about.' For a moment her beaming smile faltered. 'It started affecting our business, didn't it, Joe?'

Joe finally spoke. 'She was very down. We both were.'

'It was an adoption agency that suggested we think about China,' Lola said, brightening. 'It's not something we'd have even thought of.'

Joe and Lola had just touched down from Beijing, where they'd been able to adopt a baby girl, who was currently sitting on her dad's lap, looking up at me with a beaming smile.

'The baby's nationality didn't come into it for us,' Joe said.

'All children need love and there are so many unwanted ones out there, right?' Lola added.

'No arguments from me there,' I said, patting my now rather large tummy. 'I think it's a wonderful thing.'

In the late 1970s, the Chinese government had introduced a one-child policy to help reduce the birth rate and slow the growth of the nation's population. Where previous governments had encouraged big families to increase the workforce, the current one felt that the rates of population growth were becoming unmanageable. The policy meant that each couple was allowed just one child, with education and childcare benefits afforded to those who followed the rule. Those who didn't follow the rule received no benefits and were fined. One of the biggest problems with this policy was that, traditionally, Chinese families had a preference for boys rather than girls, so large numbers of little girls ended up without families. At the start of the new millennium, it was reported that 90 per cent of aborted foetuses in China were female and there were even some cases of baby girls being murdered at birth.

The policy also meant that there were a large number of female children and babies in Chinese orphanages, leading to many western adoption agencies concentrating on babies from there. I know this happened in India too, but I only saw those from China. It wasn't a particularly fast process and prospective parents often spent three or four months in China sorting out adoption papers and legalities before they could bring their new babies home. Usually, the children were about six to nine months old when they arrived.

Today, my job was to give Lola and Joe's baby – this new UK citizen – a quick health check, just like anybody else coming from a country where TB was endemic. We didn't, however, X-ray babies or anyone under the age of sixteen because we didn't want to expose children or infants to the radiation. On a transatlantic flight a passenger is already exposed to more cosmic radiation than they would be during a chest X-ray simply due to the few hours spent at 38,000 feet, and we didn't want to add to that exposure for children. With new babies coming in from China, all I could do was examine them, which I did at a rate of about one each month during the time those adoptions were happening. They'd already had a thorough health check before being allowed to leave the country, so by the time they got to us they were just bonny and healthy, and it really was the happiest part of my job. That day, Lola and Joe were overjoyed with their little girl, and who could blame them? This child, with dark, spiky hair and moon-like cheeks, was totally scrumptious and once the examination was over, all I wanted to do was scoop her up and cuddle her.

'Can I, Joe? Do you mind? She's just so gorgeous.'

Joe lifted her towards me and Lola's face lit up with delight at showing off their baby. It wasn't just me either – pretty soon all the female staff were queuing up to hug this smiling, sweet-smelling bundle. It was a wonderful moment in our world at Heathrow and made a change from checking endless chest X-rays.

Ten minutes later, Joe and Lola were on their way, carrying their new child like the most precious of parcels. They'd clearly been through the wringer with all the difficulties of not being able to conceive, and failed attempts at IVF, so seeing them walking out of the unit so happily was a real lift. So many of the cases I dealt with on a daily basis at HCU were grim, but this was a real pleasure.

Sadly, even before the one-child policy in China came to an end, the Chinese government put a stop to the adoption of Chinese orphans and unwanted babies by western families, which to me was a real shame. Perhaps, for the government, it felt too much like a racket, selling their babies off to foreign families. There was also the ongoing debate as to whether it was a good idea for western or European families to bring up Asian children in a different culture. While I understood the argument and appreciated the potential difficulties involved, the adopted Chinese babies I came into contact with at HCU went – as far as I could tell – to good homes where they'd be very much loved. To me, that was the most important thing. Seeing new parents like Lola and Joe with their new babies was a highlight of my job at Heathrow.

# 10

# manning the borders

ATTENDING PATIENTS with potentially infectious diseases on board flights was a big part of my job, and undoubtedly where I was under the most pressure to make exactly the right decision. Great Britain being an island, Port Health was responsible for the initial containment of any particularly nasty diseases like influenza or Ebola, thus minimizing the risk of their spreading to the whole country. Although the most common diseases I came across were chickenpox and malaria, I also dealt with some of the more serious infections in my time at Heathrow, including typhoid and rabies.

It was on a bright morning in 2005 when a worried-sounding ground crew member called HCU, just as I'd grabbed a cup of coffee and was about to take the weight off for ten minutes.

'Dr Green, we've got a suspected case of bird flu on a BA flight from China which is about to land.'

'Bird flu?'

My stomach did a quick somersault. It's not as if these words were entirely unexpected – it was more a case of when than if – or that I wasn't ready to act upon them, but the media furore around this virus was in full swing and as all the medical staff at Heathrow were on alert, it was damn near impossible not to get swept up in it and, with the Secretary of State for Health referring to 'extra checks at the borders', we at HCU were feeling the pressure even more.

First off, the plane had to be kept well away from the terminal buildings.

'Right,' I said, 'you need to tell the pilot to park in a side area off the runway until I've decided what's going on. I'll drive out and meet the plane.'

'All clear, Doctor,' the crewman said.

A young woman had been taken ill mid-flight with flu-like symptoms, which wouldn't necessarily have been so worrying had the plane not arrived from China where the epidemic was currently rife. On top of that, the passenger had intimated to a crew member that she might well have come in contact with the virus. These two facts were pivotal in my decision to keep the aircraft close to the runway on which it had landed, rather than letting it taxi to the stand. And obviously nobody was allowed to disembark, not even the pilot. I didn't want 350 people dispersing to the four corners of the UK and beyond, taking avian flu along with them. This was potentially very serious and, as the plane was not coming to the terminal building, I was going to have to get into my car and drive out to meet it.

As far as pandemics go, there were three major crises during my time at Heathrow. There was SARS (severe acute respiratory syndrome) in 2002–03, avian influenza (commonly known as bird flu) in 2005 and swine influenza in 2009–10. They could all be pretty nasty and, like most viruses, there aren't many specific treatment options other than supportive measures: rest, plenty of fluids and paracetamol to treat fever and pain. The UK has also stockpiled various anti-viral medications, for example Tamiflu, but the overall efficacy of such drugs in bird flu in particular is unproven. Usually, it's just a matter of waiting until the affected patient has cleared the virus themselves. These three viruses had all caused epidemics in their countries of origin, so our government was very keen to minimize transmission within the UK.

Swine flu is actually the common name for the H1N1 virus, so called because it has a similar form to the virus seen in pigs. In truth, it's no more dangerous than the other influenzas that strike in winter, but it can be serious for people with existing long-term health conditions or who are undergoing treatment such as chemotherapy. The 2009–10 outbreak was the last big epidemic during my time at Heathrow, and was initially found in Central and South America. Port Health would meet all flights from affected countries, board them at the stand and address the passengers, checking if anyone had been in contact with someone who had been exposed to the virus, or if anyone had shown signs or symptoms of the condition during the flight.

I'd always have a couple of HCOs on hand who would tear up and down the aisle taking temperatures, and if there were any over 38°C we'd take the passenger back to HCU for further investigation. We also handed out leaflets with information about what someone should do if they were to develop symptoms – for example, don't go to your local doctor or A&E department and sit in a room with fifty other people to whom you might pass it on. Instead, call your GP so you can be assessed at home or in a side room, if required. Obvious stuff, which often needed hammering home. The other thing about swine flu was that it really was a disease of the poorer areas, where people might live in close proximity to their animals, so many of the people who suffered from it in Central and South America weren't the kind of people who would have been flying to the UK. It was essentially something you caught from pigs, with only very limited human-to-human transmission so it was less likely to be passed on to tourists or business travellers.

With the H5N1 bird flu epidemic of 2005, there was a bit more general anxiety. For a start, it was a more serious condition, plus there had been a huge amount of press and publicity about it, globally. The good news as far as bird flu was concerned was that it didn't infect people easily and wasn't generally transmitted from human to human, but there had been some cases of human infection, sometimes with fatal consequences. Geese, chickens, ducks and turkeys are all candidates for the virus, which can be passed between farm or wild birds and even pets. Many birds with the infection don't actually get sick, so the virus can be quite insidious, posing an unseen risk to people who come into contact with them.

The symptoms, which can come on very suddenly, range from a fever, headaches and high temperature to more serious conditions like diarrhoea and vomiting, pains in the chest and bleeding from the nose and gums. The incubation period is usually three to five days, although in some cases it can be longer, but the most significant thing about avian flu is that within days of symptoms appearing, potentially fatal complications like pneumonia, severe respiratory problems and even multiple organ failure can develop. It's absolutely vital that somebody who's contracted the virus receives prompt medical advice and treatment with antiviral medication, if required.

So that morning when I was told about a suspected case of bird flu, I gulped down my coffee and got my act together. It was time to don my doctor's superhero get-up: white paper jump suit, facemask and the whole protective kit. In this head-to-toe ensemble, I looked more like some massive, weird snowman than a trustworthy medical professional. I wasn't wildly keen on wearing it at the best of times because I felt a bit ridiculous. For one thing, it always felt quite melodramatic: me rocking up, swathed in protective gear, and on top of that I worried I must frighten the passengers, lumbering into the confines of a plane cabin, all done up like something out of *CSI: Miami*. As a doctor, one tends to do one's best not to scare people if it's at all avoidable. At least I do. The other thing about these suits was, because they were paper, I'd invariably put my foot through a couple and have to start all over again before I actually managed to get one on.

Nonetheless, I wasn't taking any chances. Bird flu was a serious illness and I'd be lying if I said that I wasn't keen to avoid it. The bird flu panic wasn't long after I'd returned from my first maternity leave, and our son Henry was not even a year old. Not surprisingly, being a mother had changed how I felt about the infections and illnesses I encountered every day at Heathrow. Henry was safely at home with his dad now, walking the dogs round the farm or the park, but the next morning I'd be back home kissing and cuddling them both.

However unlikely it was that I was going to catch something and pass it on, flashes of anxiety were inevitable.

In fact, bird flu was such a hot topic of concern that I suggested that the HCOs Mandy and June stay the other side of the plane door that morning. They could wait safely outside, and if I needed them for surveillance at any point they would be right there. As far as I was concerned, the fewer people who were exposed to any potential danger, the better. Today the responsibility for making a diagnosis and recommending treatment was mine and mine alone, and as the three of us drove towards the runway, I felt unusually edgy.

By the time I arrived at the plane, the passengers had already been alerted that there was sickness on board. They'd also been informed that nobody was allowed to disembark until the all-clear was given. I climbed the stairs and banged on the door, and the second it was open I'd stepped aboard and it was closed tightly behind me.

Given the hysteria in the preceding months about bird flu, it was understandable that the passengers on board weren't especially keen on the idea of being cooped up in a confined space with somebody who was displaying its symptoms. That said, you'd be surprised at the percentage of passengers who, when faced with the chance of being exposed to a highly infectious disease, will happily waltz off the plane and take their chances, killer virus or not. As time went on, I discovered that people were often more concerned about missing their onward flight than catching something awful.

Of course many of the passengers on this flight were Chinese. The Chinese had long been advocates of protective mask wearing in crowded or confined areas where they might be susceptible to picking up nasty germs, and as I looked around the plane I saw men, women and children with their noses and mouths covered with disposable cotton. The truth is, these kinds of masks have a very limited window of efficacy and are only made for very short-term use. As soon as your breath moistens and warms them up, they're rendered pretty ineffective, a fact to which I'm fairly certain most of the people wearing them were oblivious.

The sick passenger was a woman called Jennifer who looked to be in her forties, and I was surprised to discover that she was British, not Chinese, as I'd imagined. As I approached her seat, Jennifer smiled nervously up at me. I noticed the whips of her brunette hair stuck to her moist skin and droplets of sweat gathering above her top lip, the red rims of her eyes and her pallor.

'Hi, Jennifer, I'm Dr Green. Can you tell me what's happened? Any fever, cough, sore throat?'

'All of the above I'm afraid, Doctor,' she said. 'Do you think I have it?'

'It's hard to say without checking you over properly,' I said.

She was still in the midst of all the other passengers and the ones closest to her were looking decidedly uncomfortable. What else could the crew have done? There was nowhere to put her. Sometimes, when a passenger is taken ill, the crew might move them up into first class so they can lie down and be more comfortable, but there was no way that was going to happen in this particular case. Let's face it, any passenger who'd shelled all that cash for a first-class seat was going to be more than a little miffed if a member of cabin crew sauntered up to them saying, 'Excuse me, madam, would you mind if this lady with suspected bird flu took the adjacent seat?' So that was out.

I felt awful looming over this poor woman, clad in all my protective gear, and she must have felt mortified as well as extremely anxious because all eyes were on us. She was compos mentis but looked thoroughly exhausted and not at all well, shivering and wrapped up in a couple of airline blankets.

'How long had you been in China, Jennifer?' I asked.

'I work in Fujian Province,' she said. 'I'm there most of the time. I'm travelling home to visit my family.'

'And how long have you been feeling like this?'

'Just a few hours really,' she said. 'I had a bit of a cough and sore throat earlier but I was OK when I boarded the flight.'

'And what makes you think you might have come in contact with the virus?'

Jennifer winced, as if she were dreading the question. 'There's a market near where I live, with lots of live birds. I walk through it every day on the way to work and I did hear that a lot of birds had to be slaughtered because of the outbreak.' She looked up at me, searching for reassurance. 'It's not like I handled the birds or anything.' Then her face fell. 'There was also a colleague who was diagnosed with bird flu and I did do some work with him, but I didn't think it was a person-to-person disease so I didn't think I was at risk.'

Of course she was right; there had been very few documented cases of human-to-human transmission of the disease, so the chances of her having caught it from a work colleague were fairly slim. But there had been some contact, and I knew it was not impossible. As a doctor at Heathrow, I'd been bestowed with the responsibility of protecting the borders from this horrible illness, so in the present climate I couldn't rule out anything.

I could feel Jennifer's eyes on me as I took her temperature, which at 39°C was a high fever. A quick burst of coughing sent her violently forward in the chair, and a woman on the opposite side of the aisle clapped her hand over her mouth. Once the coughing had subsided, I asked her to remove the blankets so I could listen to her chest. Of course, I couldn't have her take off her shirt in front of all the other passengers, but it was flimsy enough that I could use the stethoscope through the fabric.

'Now lean forward, please,' I said.

I listened to the base of her lungs, which sounded OK, but a quick check of her tongue suggested she might be dehydrated. I checked her capillary refill time, which involves taking the pulp, or fleshy part, of the finger and pushing it until it blanches, and then checking how long it takes for the skin colour to return to normal. It should take two seconds, but Jennifer's took more like four. She needed fluids.

'What do you think, Doctor?' she said. 'You think I have it, don't you?'

'Well, we certainly need to get you checked out, Jennifer,' I said, 'but to be honest it's more probable that you just have a nasty cold that's given you a temperature, sore throat and cough.'

I always try to put people at ease and to focus on a positive outcome rather than what the worst-case scenario might be.

'Really?'

'Look, it's almost impossible to distinguish bird flu from any other flu, initially,' I assured her. 'We can only do it by a blood test.'

It was true; there was no way to tell. We just had to use our judgement and weigh up the facts of the story surrounding the patient. If she'd been chopping up dead birds in a market, the likelihood of her having it would have been much stronger.

'We do have to be on the safe side, though, so I am going to have to get you to hospital to be checked over and tested. Does that sound OK?'

She nodded, looking up at me stoically, just as one of her fellow passengers spoke up.

'Is there any danger to us if she does have bird flu, Doctor?'

It was a man in his mid-forties, speaking from the row of seats behind.

'There really is very little chance of person-to-person transmission, sir,' I said.

'But it's not impossible?' his female companion asked hesitantly.

'Very, very slim,' I reiterated firmly. 'But I'll be checking everyone, and anyone with any worries can speak to me as they disembark from the plane.'

Their concerns were completely understandable, especially with all the sensational press and media attention. I looked back at Jennifer, who was shrinking as far down into her seat as she could possibly manage.

'You'll be fine, Jennifer,' I said. 'Let's just get you looked over properly, eh?'

Glancing over my shoulder, I signalled to the purser that I needed to talk to her privately.

'We need to call the paramedics and get them over here,' I said quietly. 'This woman needs to go to hospital for some tests, but let's do it with the least fuss possible.'

The purser nodded and did what she needed to do, while I headed to the front of the cabin to make an announcement over the speaker system – another of my top five least favourite things about this job.

'Ladies and gentlemen, could I have your attention please?' I recoiled at the sound of my amplified voice booming through the aircraft like a harridan. Back then I hated any kind of public speaking: my voice always shook and I felt so exposed. Still, I soldiered on.

'We've had what might be a case of bird flu on the flight. Please don't be alarmed. It could just as well be a regular virus, but in the current situation we have to check all possibilities so disembarkation might be a while longer.'

I've been on flights that have been a nightmare, with people jumping up and opening the overhead lockers and not paying any attention to what I'm saying at all, but today I just saw a sea of faces blinking at me with what I took to be wretched discontentment.

'If you can just bear with us, thank you.'

As I mentioned, the behaviour of the passengers seemed to depend on how much control the crew wielded on a particular airline. Although the BA and Virgin crews always seemed to have it together, on some airlines a simple request for everyone to remain in their seats and wait before getting up to collect their bags from the overhead lockers could go ignored, and to expect any sort of help from the flight attendants was futile. I recall one occasion, when I was fighting my way down the aisle of a flight from Dubai to get to a man who'd been taken ill mid-flight, where, despite my strident request over the speaker system that everybody remain seated, I was virtually trampled underfoot.

In the eye of the mayhem I caught the attention of a stewardess who was standing in one of the galleys observing the action.

'Could you just keep them in their seats for a little while longer, please?'

The woman smiled and nodded, but seemed to have no ability – or inclination – to exert any authority over the passengers.

Once I realized I was on my own, I got stroppy.

'Look! I cannot deal with the situation unless you do as I ask,' I said, loudly and firmly. 'If you want to get off this flight then I need to attend to the sick passenger and I cannot do that if you are all blocking the aisle.'

A fair few of the passengers completely ignored me and the crew made no attempt to come to my rescue and settle people back in their seats, but in the end I managed to exert enough authority to make my way to the sick passenger and move things along.

In the case of Jennifer, she was showing signs of something that could very well have been bird flu, so now I was going to have to check in with everyone on the plane and that was going to take a while. I had no choice. I certainly had no intention of being the doctor who missed it and let the virus run riot in the UK. It had now been a couple of hours since the plane had landed so everyone was pretty exhausted. I felt like 90 per cent of them couldn't care less whether they had bird flu or not, they just wanted to get off the damn plane, have a shower and continue on their journey, but I had a job to do. I wanted to get through the process quickly but not at the expense of being thorough. It wasn't long before the ambulance arrived and Jennifer was taken off to hospital, all under the watchful gaze of the other passengers who remained relatively calm. Mandy and June then came aboard, checking all the forms had been filled out with contact details, etc. The passengers were also issued with instructions on what to do if they suddenly showed symptoms, and there was a contact number to call if that were the case.

It's funny, I always worried about scaring the passengers in this kind of situation, but it was amazing how sanguine the people on that flight were at the sight of me boarding in full protective gear. Throughout the bird flu crisis I found that many of the Chinese passengers, even though they came from the epicentre of the epidemic, seemed to think it wasn't going to affect them. They saw it as someone else's problem. It was a case of 'so what!' They'd lived with the threat in China anyway, so it didn't seem like a big deal. Still, on that Thursday morning I stood at the door of the plane so I could answer any queries or worries as people filed past me off the flight.

A young British woman stopped as she passed me. 'I'm six months pregnant and I was just two rows behind the sick woman,' she said. 'Do you think it will affect my baby?'

I'd spotted this girl while I was talking to Jennifer and she seemed OK, but now she looked terrified, probably due to the activity that had been going on around her.

'Please don't worry, the chances of catching bird flu from two rows back are extremely remote,' I said, putting my hand on her arm. 'If you do have any symptoms at all, do call your midwife or your GP straight away, but I think you'll be fine.'

Arriving back at Terminal 3, I peeled off the white paper suit and mask and disposed of them.

'How did it go, Stephanie?' Megan said, handing me a coffee. 'Do you think she had bird flu?'

'They'll only know for sure with a blood test, but it's possible, poor thing,' I said. I flopped down in a chair feeling decidedly sweaty myself. 'She lived near a market where lots of birds had to be slaughtered because of it, so . . .'

'Oh, that's a nuisance,' Megan said, always the master of understatement.

I puffed out a sigh and then took a healthy glug of my much-needed coffee. 'It's hard to know what to think, to be honest. Part of me thinks it's unlikely she has it, but then I only have to think about the number of flights coming into Heathrow every day and it just feels like a matter of time before I find a patient who does.'

Later that afternoon, I called Hillingdon Hospital to follow up on Jennifer. Although most of the time we're not party to the outcome of the cases, this was different. If I had just dealt with my first case of avian flu I wanted to know about it, and I knew Dr Thana would too. When the lab at the hospital told me she was clear, the rush of relief through my body surprised me. On a daily basis, I did my best to push all the stress and worry deep down because that's the best way I knew of dealing with it. I told myself that all this epidemic stuff was just business as usual and part of my everyday job – we had it under control. Still, on the occasions I was faced with the real possibility of it, I was always anxious that I had handled things correctly.

It was our practice at HCU to document everything, as would any GP. Aside from reviewing chest X-rays, which were reported on line, we had to document any contact we had with anyone and list all the medical details of the case. This information had to be written down as jargon-free as possible in one of several books. We had a book for immigration queries, another for infectious diseases, and so on. During the swine flu epidemic things ramped up and I was required to deliver a daily report for Dr Thana to feed back to the Health Protection Agency, which was our governing body and the public health branch of the NHS. The reports had to detail any activity or potential cases and whatever the outcome of those cases had been. This was so the Health Minister had all the correct facts and figures. In fact, by the time the swine flu epidemic was in full swing, we were under a fair bit of scrutiny. Then there was the constant stream of journalists and media people calling us and demanding answers to questions we weren't authorized to answer. Mercifully, no one from the media was allowed into HCU, but one morning I did have to deal with a pushy guy from a tabloid newspaper, inadvertently passed to me by one of the HCOs who'd taken the call at the front desk.

'Can you tell me precisely what these extra checks are that are supposed to protect the public, Dr Green?'

The guy had caught me completely off guard. 'Actually, you've come through to the wrong person.'

We'd recently been given the phone number of where to direct this kind of enquiry, and luckily I was armed with it.

'Well, you're a doctor at Heathrow, aren't you?' he said. 'Surely you can answer a simple question? What are the procedures as far as this swine flu epidemic is concerned? I think people have a right to know, don't you?'

'Look, I can give you a number for the communications team who are dealing with questions from the media, but I can't . . .'

The guy hung up on me before I'd even finished my sentence. He probably already had the number of the communications team but was trying to get the dirt straight from the horse's mouth – chancing his arm. It was only recently that the Health Protection Agency had taken over responsibility for the unit and they had given us numbers to pass media enquiries on to. Before that it had been very ad hoc and was down to us on the ground to deal with, without any real support or guidance. By the time swine flu hit the headlines there was a realisation that the situation could garner very negative headlines if the powers that be weren't on top of it.

This epidemic felt very stressful and we, the doctors, hated the additional pressure. Anyone coming into the country with a fever became a potential carrier and people came into the unit with fever all the time. Whether it was a case of malaria or just a case of good old-fashioned diarrhoea and vomiting, thorough health history checks had to be made and the passengers needed to be examined. And with the extra task of meeting and stringent checking of all the Mexican flights as a matter of course every day, our workload doubled. We were on high alert.

If I'm honest, I fretted about these high-profile epidemics in any number of ways: had I made the right decision with a passenger I'd seen? Was malaria the right diagnosis and was I sure it wasn't something else? And worst of all, what if somebody did slip through the net with one of these nasty viruses on my watch and there was a subsequent outbreak? What then? I was the backstop for anything sinister that might arrive at the airport, and besides the epidemics I had a real fear of letting through something even worse, like the Ebola virus. I had a terrible nagging anxiety of getting it wrong. Making a bad call. And in moments of stress, I'd play the headlines in my mind: 'Heathrow Doctor Misses Case of Marburg Virus' or a hundred others. I certainly didn't want that to be the only thing I was ever known for, and there was an ever-present whisper, telling me that I mustn't, under any circumstances, screw it up.

The day before our second child Wilf was born, Chris sold the Trout. He'd recently taken on another pub, the Radnor Arms in a village called Coleshill that's owned wholly by the National Trust. Being a Trust pub, it wasn't for sale but Chris had taken over the lease to run it, sort out the food and generally jazz it up a bit. Not long after Chris had started to make his mark at the Radnor, his business partner in the Trout decided he too wanted to move to his own pub, which is why they had to sell the Trout. This sale turned into a major upheaval as it was a huge pub with lots of rooms, and Chris would often have to be on hand to show prospective new owners around while trying to manage the Radnor. It was eventually sold for a decent price, and ended a stressful period for us both.

Our children were born just shy of two years apart: Henry in October 2004 and Wilf in June 2006, so I'd been back at work less than a year before I was on maternity leave again. I'd managed to remain in blissful ignorance about what was going on at Heathrow during my periods of leave, particularly the first. Like many new mums-to-be I'd met, I was incredibly self-absorbed in the last couple of months of my pregnancy, and once Henry was born I was completely wrapped up in him. There was such a wonderful freedom, just concentrating on Henry and being a mum. Initially, I couldn't even think about work simply because I found having a new baby so overwhelming. I certainly couldn't imagine going back to work and combining the two things, even though I always knew I would. So apart from Jane, whom I'd sometimes seen with Henry on her days off, I didn't keep in touch with anyone from work. With Wilf, I was similarly detached from my life at Heathrow, but by then I knew that it was possible to combine motherhood and career because I'd already managed it with Henry.

After a few days being back at work after Wilf, I came to the conclusion that going to work and dealing with sickness and death might be construed as light relief compared with coping with a toddler and a baby full time. Blessed freedom, in fact! I mean, at work I could go to the loo all on my own without a small child trailing after me or without the worry of having to leap-up, mid-flow, and dash to the call of a screaming infant with my jeans around my knees. I could drink a whole, hot cup of coffee uninterrupted, or leaf through a magazine that wasn't covered in breakfast or drool or worse.

I'd missed the full-on human drama of Heathrow's HCU, and no sooner was I back than I was up to my neck again.

'Steph, I'm so happy you're back but God, you've missed a lot of excitement!'

Jane beckoned me into the rest room the minute I walked into HCU and put the kettle on. We'd seen a fair bit of each other while in I was on maternity leave, but it was great to be back at work together.

'What have I missed? What excitement?' I said.

I was raring to get stuck in after months of just doing mum-type things with only a toddler and a baby for company, so I hated the thought that I'd missed out on something juicy that I could have really got my teeth into. That said, I was pretty certain it couldn't have been anything that I hadn't already dealt with or seen a hundred times before. On this occasion I was wrong.

'It's all gone a bit James Bond around here this week,' Mandy said, joining in the conversation. 'Quite scary really.'

'Why?'

'Suspected radiation contamination on flights, especially those from Moscow,' Jane said.

A moment to digest the news . . . 'Oh, right. I see.'

Jane continued, telling me that Health Protection Agency staff had been boarding aircraft with Geiger counters to check for traces of radiation as soon as they'd landed. 'All flights from Russia are being checked,' she said.

This wasn't long after the poisoning of Russian dissident Alexander Litvinenko in November 2006, which had been all over the media. In fact, you'd have had to have been living under a rock not to have heard about it, but I'd been so ensconced on 'planet baby' that I hadn't really considered how it was going to affect us at Port Health.

'So have they found anything?' I asked.

'No,' she said. 'I think they're trying to find out whether the substance that killed Litvinenko came over on a flight into Heathrow.'

It wasn't hard to imagine how worrying it must have been for incoming passengers knowing that the plane they'd just flown in on was being checked for traces of potentially lethal radiation, especially as Immigration were then ferrying them all off the plane and straight into a holding area. There the HCOs filled out quarantine cards for each individual and explained the symptoms and effects of radiation poisoning and what to look out for. They were told that if they became ill with any of these symptoms while in the country, they were to act immediately and seek medical help.

There had been a couple of similar incidents handled by colleagues during my time at Heathrow. I recalled a period early on when a suspicious white powder was found on board a few flights landing at Terminal 4 and anthrax was suspected.

Anthrax is a bacterial disease in sheep and cattle, affecting the skin and lungs, but it can also be passed to humans, who have cold or flu-like symptoms for several days before pneumonia and severe respiratory collapse, which often proves fatal. The bacteria can also be grown in laboratories. In 2001, in Washington, Florida and New York, five people died in bioterrorism attacks when they inhaled airborne spores or touched a powder form of anthrax that was contained in letters delivered by the US Postal Service.

There was also one flight from the USA that Port Health was alerted to because five or six passengers seated at the rear of the plane had actually fainted. On that occasion it had been a team of firemen who were sent on board to check it out, and the cause was found to be carbon dioxide used as a coolant. Some of the boxes containing the coolant had been fractured and the gas had escaped from the cargo section of the flight into the passenger deck.

This latest situation was far more serious, and one of the most explosive stories to emerge while I was Heathrow. It was alleged that two KGB members had been sent over to murder Litvinenko with polonium-210, which is astronomically more deadly than hydrogen cyanide and, when swallowed or inhaled, is one of the most toxic poisons known. On top of that, polonium-210 has a long half-life – which is the period of time required for the concentration or amount of a substance to be reduced by one-half – and it always leaves a trail.

While I've been writing this book a similar story has erupted with the poisoning of former Russian spy Sergei Skripal and his daughter Yulia, who appear to have been poisoned with a nerve agent developed in Russia. This time the UK government has clearly demonstrated that they suspect the Russian authorities and expelled twenty-three of their diplomats; dozens of other countries have expelled Russian envoys in solidarity with the UK. But how was the nerve agent transported into the country?

After the Litvinenko case, British Airways reported that two planes at Heathrow had been found to have traces of a radioactive substance present, and the airline subsequently had to make contact with passengers who'd travelled on over 200 flights to Europe and Moscow – around 30,000 people in total. Can you imagine that many people potentially affected? The numbers were staggering and it really brought home to all of us who were assigned to protect UK ports just how catastrophic something like this might have been.

## 11

# stranger things

SOME DAYS WORKING for Port Health were stranger than others, and this one started on a freezing winter morning early in 2007. It was one of those mornings when I got stuck behind a bus-load of flight crew at the control post. I hated those mornings. Now I was going to have to wait for each and every one of them to be checked through security: pilots, co-pilots, stewards and stewardesses with all their bags. And, given that looking good is part of the job description for most of the crew, that meant a lot of make-up, potions and lotions. Literally everything had to be checked, and watching them slowly unload their gear on to the conveyor belt triggered my impatient Type-A personality every time.

When my turn finally came, I jumped out of my car, grabbed my bags off the back seat and loaded them on to the belt that would carry them through the scanner, then I walked through the body scanner, smiling affably at the security men as I went. Nothing unusual. I did the same thing every day without issue. But not today.

As soon I was through the scanner, Elias, one of the few security staff I knew by name, approached me with a strange look in his eye.

'Dr Green, do you have any idea what's in the boot of your car?'

'There's nothing in the boot of my car,' I said with confidence, remembering that I'd cleaned everything out of it the previous afternoon.

'Isn't there?'

'Well . . . no . . . is there?' Suddenly I wasn't so sure.

'I think you'd better come and have a look,' he said.

He looked deadly serious and I was momentarily filled with dread. Following him back to the open boot of my car, I looked down.

'Oh . . .'

I was staring down at what might have been the tools of a meticulous serial killer: a carvery of knives of varying shapes, sizes and hazard. They were all neatly stored in a leather bag, which Elias had opened.

'Oh no!'

'Oh no what, Dr Green?' he said. 'Somebody has planted bad ass weapons in your car?'

'No,' I said. I could feel myself blushing. 'It's my husband who . . .'

'Oh?'

'He's a chef and . . .' I considered several possibilities. 'Yes. He was the last one to use my car and he's obviously left his chef's knives in the boot.'

'Chef's knives?' Elias said, like I was making it up.

'Yes, my husband has just forgotten to take them.'

I was saying it but I couldn't quite believe that Chris had actually done it, knowing the security hoops I had to jump through on a daily basis.

'Well, I'm sure you understand that I can't let you take them through, Dr Green,' Elias said.

'Really? Not even if I just leave them in the boot?'

Elias snorted. 'How do I know what you're going to do with them?'

'Well, I assume you've seen enough of me to know that I'm not about to dash on board an A320 brandishing a boning knife and demanding that they fly me to Bora Bora,' I said.

His eyes widened and I found myself wishing I hadn't said that. In the wrong hands, these babies could do some serious damage.

'Let me just make a quick phone call,' I said.

I phoned Chris, who, rather than apologizing for causing me such grief first thing in the morning, sounded wholly irked by the situation.

'What do you mean you have to leave them at the control post?' he said. 'Steph, please don't leave my knives there. They're really valuable. They're my work tools.'

'I know they're really valuable, Chris, that's why I'm slightly baffled as to why you left them in my bloody car.'

'Obviously I just forgot,' he said.

'You know full well I have to drive through a strictly controlled area every morning,' I said. 'And now I've got a security officer who thinks I'm a serial killer.'

Out of the corner of my eye, I could see Elias and another officer sniggering like schoolboys as they took the leather bag out of the boot of my car. I was mortified. Now I'd have to come back and collect the knives on the way home that evening, which was really annoying as it was a completely different route on the way out.

As I drove through the second gates, airside, I muttered to myself. 'I'll kill him. I'll bloody kill him.'

It wasn't the last time I'd have to go through this rigmarole, but it was generally my own fault. After my children were born, I attempted to drive through the control post with a forgotten buggy in the boot on countless occasions. If the guard on duty was of the more thorough variety, I'd have to lug the thing out of the boot and drag it through the scanner along with all the rest of my overnight bags and anything else I had with me. It was understandable, I suppose, a child's buggy being made up of hollow tubes in which it was possible to carry anything.

I hadn't been in my office for more than five minutes after the knife debacle when Mandy and June were upon me.

'There's blood all over one of the baggage carousels, Stephanie,' Mandy said, wide-eyed.

'I'm sorry, did you say blood?' Surely I couldn't have heard right.

'Blood, yes,' Mandy said. 'One of the luggage supervisors alerted us so we had a quick look. It's pouring out of a suitcase and it's all over the belt.'

'I'd have said leaking rather than pouring,' June said, spoiling Mandy's moment somewhat.

'And are you absolutely sure it's blood?' I said.

'Well, it's red,' Mandy said, her voice a drama-filled stage whisper.

'It's probably Ribena,' June muttered.

Mandy threw her a look. 'I don't think so, June.'

They were an odd pairing, these two, but always good value. Mandy – a dead ringer for Naomi Campbell – hailed from Dominica. She stood at about five feet eleven and always wore heels. By contrast June, her regular sidekick, was a tiny grey-haired Scottish lady who smoked like a factory chimney. June was one of those people who always had an irreverent joke or a cutting line up her sleeve. She and Mandy were always fun to be around.

'Is the baggage carousel still in use?' I asked.

'It was still going round when I looked, with people just staring down at it,' June said. 'The supervisors wondered if you'd pop down and have a look.'

'Me? Why me? The baggage hall isn't in our jurisdiction; we're not supposed to be dealing with it,' I said. 'The supervisors need to stop any more luggage being loaded on to the belt and to stop the belt if hasn't already been done. And tell them to keep people away from it. Don't let anyone touch it.'

'So are you going down there or not?' June said.

'No, June. It's nothing to do with us,' I said.

The problem with this point-blank refusal was that I was actually dying to know what it was, so five minutes later I was striding through the airport with Mandy towards Baggage Reclaim, on the pretext of being on a coffee break. It crossed my mind that I probably should have been wearing my protective gear. It was blood, after all. Too late now, we were on our way.

By the time we arrived, the suspect Samsonite was the only case left on the belt and, indeed, seeping macabrely out of it was something that very much resembled blood. I got closer. Yes, it was definitely blood, but whose? Or what's? Should I just open it up then and there? At least I'd know what I was dealing with.

'Where did you say the flight had come from?' I asked a hovering baggage supervisor.

'Kenya,' she said. 'Direct from Mombasa.'

'And nobody has turned up to claim it?'

She shook her head. I urged her to keep everyone well back and away from the case, whilst I pulled on a pair of surgical gloves I'd found in my handbag. Then I slowly began to unzip it. No locks, thank goodness. Whoever had taken this strange cargo on to a plane couldn't have been all that worried that someone might go through it. As I peeled back the top of the case, a pungent smell hit me. Inside, there was a lot of screwed-up newspaper, an empty plastic water bottle and a large paper parcel from which the blood was seeping.

'God, is that some sort of meat?' I said, stepping back.

'Oh, that's horrible,' Mandy said.

Hands gloved, I pulled open the parcel, revealing what looked like a furless, mutilated animal of some sort. Not nice. Whatever it was, it hadn't been particularly well wrapped either.

The baggage officer appeared over my shoulder and grimaced. 'What is that?'

I peered downward for a closer exploration. 'Do you

know, I think it's some sort of monkey,' I said. 'I think it's a chopped-up monkey.'

'I think I'm going to be sick,' Mandy gasped.

The baggage supervisor rolled her eyes as if she wasn't the least bit surprised at seeing a chopped-up monkey going around on an airport luggage carousel, and she probably wasn't. People tried to bring all sorts of strange things through customs and she'd probably seen it all before.

'Bush meat?' I said, and the baggage supervisor nodded.

Illegal bush meats were big business and tons of it were smuggled into Britain each year: monkey, gorilla, camel, crocodile, elephant. You name it and somebody has a taste for it. The danger was that it posed a disease risk to our own cattle and other farm animals.

'I wonder why nobody came to collect it?' Mandy said. 'Someone obviously brought this over for a reason.'

I peered into the case, nose wrinkled. 'I reckon they got to the carousel, saw the blood and thought better of it. I mean, you wouldn't want to wheel a case through the "Nothing To Declare" exit trailing blood behind you, would you?'

Mandy and the baggage supervisor nodded in agreement, and I suggested that it be handed over to customs. The baggage supervisor would arrange decontamination and deep cleaning of the luggage belt. I headed back to HCU, wondering if the morning could get any weirder.

The answer was yes. Back at HCU, my next patient was already waiting for me in one of the cubicles: a middle-aged Dutch guy, straight off a flight from Kuala Lumpar. He was holding his groin, in a lot of pain.

'OK, what's going on?' I said. 'Can you tell me exactly where the pain is so I can check you over?'

He blinked up at me as if I were mad for even asking.

'Are there no male doctors here?' he said.

'Er . . . not really,' I said, slightly taken aback. 'Why?'

He spoke through gritted teeth, almost doubled over. 'I don't want to be examined by a female doctor. I want a male doctor.'

He was a handsome, tall guy, blond and in his late forties, but his face was racked with pain. Something was very wrong here.

'What's your name?' I said.

'Daan.'

'Well, Daan, can you at least tell me what the problem is?' I said.

'I really want to see a male doctor,' he said again.

I called over to June, who was just back from her cigarette break. 'Can you give Dr Thana a call in Terminal 4, please? If he's not in the middle of something, could you ask him to head over to us?'

'I'm on it,' June said.

167

I turned back to the the man. 'OK, I've had someone call my boss and hopefully he'll be here shortly to have a look at you. In the meantime, can you at least tell me what's wrong and where the pain is?'

'It's like a sharp pain in my groin,' he said, but he wouldn't look me in the eye as he spoke.

'And when did it start?'

'Towards the end of the flight.'

After that, he pretty much clammed up, and it was impossible to diagnose anything without examining him. My first thought was that he might have a twisted testis, but a second offer to look him over didn't go down any better than the first, despite my reminder to him that he wasn't in possession of anything I hadn't seen or indeed handled before.

'I want to be seen by a man,' was all he kept saying.

June poked her head into the examination cubicle. 'Dr Thana is on his way. Five minutes tops.'

Daan was in serious pain by now and it seemed to be getting worse by the minute. I felt helpless, knowing this was something urgent but unable to help because he just wouldn't let me near him.

Five minutes later, I headed out of the cubicle, leaving him in the more than capable hands of my superior. That was the last I saw of Daan.

Dr Thana came and found me while I was on an administrative roll: finally tackling a long list of chest X-rays which needed reporting while simultaneously finishing off the enormous piece of birthday cake June had brought in for me – an ordinary moment in a *Twilight Zone* of a morning.

'How did it go with the Dutch guy?' I asked as he came into the office.

'Well, I now know why he didn't want you or any other woman examining him, Stephanie,' he said. 'He was very embarrassed, although I'm not sure if it was the afflicted area or the circumstances surrounding the condition that was causing his embarrassment.'

I looked up at him, curiously. 'Why? What's the deal with him? I thought it might be a twisted testis.'

Dr Thana sat down opposite me and shook his head. 'That's what I thought too at first, but when I examined him, his penis was painfully erect. He told me it had been like that for a while but at first he said he didn't know why.'

'OK . . .'

'I thought it might be a clot, but finally he admitted that he'd been taking a large amount of Viagra, right up until a couple of hours before he boarded the flight.'

'Gosh! So he overdosed on Viagra?'

'I've seen it before,' Dr Thana said. 'Obviously some people use Viagra as a party drug rather than just a cure for erectile dysfunction, and you can imagine what kind of parties we're talking about.'

'I'm not sure I want to while I'm eating June's birthday cake,' I said.

'I wouldn't call it an overdose exactly, but he'd had an erection for around twenty-four hours in total,' he said. 'Then eventually the pain kicked in, towards the end of the flight to London.'

'I know that in the past there have been similar cases where gangrene has set in,' he went on. Gangrene occurs when tissue is not receiving enough oxygenated blood. Dr Thana told me that an excessive amount of Viagra could lead to abnormal blood flow in the penis and surrounding areas. There had been cases where this had to led to gangrene, which had resulted in men having to have their penis amputated and subsequently reconstructed.

'I blue-lighted Daan to Hillingdon as an emergency, but I think he's OK.'

At around four that afternoon, an IO called Tom came into HCU brandishing a small bag of white tablets.

'Doctor, what are these?' He spoke with urgency, presumably thinking that I could identify any medication that's waved in front of me at close proximity.

'I have no idea,' I said, so he shoved them under my nose.

'Well, what do you think they might be?'

Tom was handsome but intense and in my head I said, 'How the hell do I know what they are?'

In the real world, I just smiled and took the bag.

'Yes, they're little white tablets with a tiny number on,' I confirmed.

'Is that all?' He was disappointed, I could tell.

'Well, that's about all I can tell you at this juncture because I don't hold a full drug repository in my head,' I said. 'What's the story with them anyway?'

'A Brazilian guy coming into the country to join his partner on a same-sex partner visa turned up with them. We'd searched his bags because his papers looked a bit iffy and we found these.'

'Do you suspect they might be narcotics?' I said.

Tom shrugged. 'He wasn't very clear about what they're for and he had no prescription for them. Obviously before we let him through we'd prefer to know if he's got some illness that's going to end up costing the NHS thousands, so we've detained him while we do a bit of digging.'

'Well, I wish I could be a bit more helpful,' I said, right before I had a light bulb moment. 'Oh hang on!'

I'd remembered an enormous book on one of the office shelves that might be of some use. (We had a lot of shelves in our office, housing hundreds of records with curly writing relating to patients going all the way back to when the first

171

plane touched down at Heathrow in the 1940s, along with a library of medical books.) When I worked there in the Noughties we had computers that were linked to the internal system at Heathrow and showed us the times and schedules of all the flights, but they weren't fully connected to the worldwide web – we could just about send an email. Today I could Google the tiny number on the tablet, but not back then. I was reliant on this huge book, which contained pictures of all the different tablets from different eras. It was colour-coded and went from little white circles to white triangles to white diamonds to pink diamonds, and so on and so forth. So perhaps I could have a go at identifying the pills, I thought. Why not? It was a quiet afternoon and it would clearly brighten up Tom's day.

So, full of enthusiasm, I dragged the great tome down from the shelf behind me and began leafing through it, brightly telling Tom that I'd get back to him as soon as I had an inkling of what they might be.

If I'd been even slightly clear-sighted I would have known that it was going to be a fool's errand from the off, chiefly because inevitably the book was already out of date and the chances of it identifying the tablets were slim to non-existent. Tablets change all the time with new formulations and new numbers, and after an hour of searching I had to admit defeat.

'I think you're going to have to give the Brazilian guy the

benefit of the doubt as without the packet I can't tell you what these are,' I told Tom over the phone.

An hour later, he was back again holding another small plastic bag, this one full of black powder.

'We've just found this tucked away in a hidden compartment in a man's case, Doctor. Can you tell us what it is?'

'No, Tom,' I said. 'I can't, but I'm pretty sure it wasn't prescribed by any doctor.' It was probably an exotic tea.

I suppose in the scheme of things the rest of that day was fairly standard but by home time, at the end of a fifteen-hour shift, I was totally whacked. By now it was 10pm and as I'd started work at 7am, I'd left the farmhouse at 5am. Not only had it been a strange day, it had been a long one and after a detour to collect Chris's knives, I had a lengthy drive home. It was minus four outside, and once I'd come off the motorway I had half an hour of driving down small, dark and treacherously icy roads. The double whammy of acute tiredness and hideous driving conditions caused me to drive so insanely slowly (and probably erratically) that I caught the attention of a passing police car and was pulled over. It had never happened to me before (and hasn't since), and on any other day it might have been a surprise but on that day it seemed par for the course. The police officer appeared at my car holding a breathalyzer, and I wound down the window, smiling weakly.

'Good evening, madam. I pulled you over because of the

extremely slow speed you were driving at,' he said. 'Are you on your way home?'

'I am,' I said, wearily. 'Look, I know I was driving at a snail's pace, officer, but I'm a doctor and I've been on a ridiculously long shift. I'm tired and I'm really worried about driving on this ice. I'm just being careful, that's all.'

The policeman peered in the window at me – work suit, no make-up, scruffy ponytail, clearly exhausted – and just smiled.

'You don't look as if you've been out having fun,' he said.

It was so blindingly obvious that I hadn't been out drinking or partying that he didn't even bother to breathalyze me, telling me instead that there wasn't all that much ice and to try to move along a little faster as travelling at such a slow speed could also be dangerous. Then he sent me on his way. As I finally headed for home I wondered what might have happened if the officer had decided to give me and the car a proper check over, opening the boot to discover my potentially deadly cargo of kitchen knives – which were hardly the tools of a doctor. I suspect then that the outcome might have been slightly different, and just like that morning; I'd have had some explaining to do.

## 12

# here comes the bride

IT WAS HOT AND SUNNY OUTSIDE, or so word had it. I couldn't actually attest to said glorious weather because I was sitting in a windowless room, somewhat exasperated, having just examined a pretty young transgender woman from Thailand for no good reason.

The IO David had brought her in, asking if I could look her over, but his objective was vague to say the least.

'I thought he might have mental issues,' he said.

'*He?*'

It struck me as odd that David thought of this person as male, but on reflection maybe he was right and I was wrong. From what I understood, some Thai transgender people identified as a 'type of male' and others 'a type of female', and some labelled themselves as a completely separate gender – a third gender. The

175

term used widely in South East Asia was 'ladyboy', especially when conversing with English-speaking people, so that was the term that I most often heard.

A few quick questions told me there was nothing mentally wrong with Achara, who was positively charming, had an aptitude for applying make-up that I could only dream of attaining, and had simply come to London for a holiday.

'So was there anything wrong I should know about?' David asked upon his return.

I giggled and shook my head. 'Well, aside from the fact that I would never have opted for floor-length peach satin as a travel outfit, I thought she was lovely.'

He blushed a little. 'So nothing, then?'

'No, there's nothing wrong with her,' I said. 'This is just her. This is how she chooses to live her life.'

This event, so far, had been my kick of excitement for the morning in amidst a stream of X-ray checking and form filling. I was just mulling it all over when Mandy popped her head around the door.

'I've been for a walk on my break,' she said. 'It's beautiful outside.'

'So I've been told by everyone who comes through here,' I said.

'You should get outside for a while and soak up a bit of sun,' she said.

'Maybe I will go out,' I said, but no sooner had the words left my lips when David was back with another pretty, young Thai woman, presumably from the same flight that Achara had come in on.

'Could we X-ray, please? She's coming in on a spouse visa,' he said.

'Of course,' I said, motioning for the young woman to come in and sit down. Her travelling companion, a much older British man, quickly joined her: pale and thin, with the few remaining wisps of hair he had swept messily across his otherwise bald pate. I suppose in another setting they might have looked like a rather odd couple, but I saw many couples just like them every week. This young woman appeared to be a mail-order bride – a woman who had listed herself in a catalogue to be selected for marriage – and the older man was her brand-new husband.

'Do you know why you're here?' I asked the woman, whose name was Prija.

She blinked at me with doe eyes but said nothing. Her husband, who looked fifty-something, introduced himself as Mr Laurie.

'I don't know why we're here,' he said. 'Perhaps you might enlighten us, Doctor.'

A tricky one, I thought. His demeanour was immediately defensive and I hadn't even started yet.

'Of course, Mr Laurie. We have to check your wife for TB as she's going to be a resident in the UK. We X-ray all new entrants who have come from countries with high levels of TB.'

'She hasn't got TB,' he said, confidently.

'Well, then, I'm sure everything's going to be fine.'

Mr Laurie and his new bride said very little to one another in the next five minutes. He sat stony-faced, slouched in his chair, while she, his timid companion, linked her arm through his, her petite hand gripping his. I found myself trying to read her: wondering if this was a display of real affection, or fear, or maybe a little of both. Like most of the Thai women I saw, Prija didn't speak much English, so her husband was going to have to do most of the talking. At least she did seem to have *some* grasp of English. Quite often I'd meet recently married couples who didn't speak one another's language at all. Perhaps all they needed was the language of love – I don't know – but I always found the concept bizarre.

Most of the Thai brides who passed through Heathrow were beautiful, innocent girls. Some of them were still teenagers, arriving in the UK for the first time with English men old enough to be their fathers and, in some cases, grandfathers. It was always quite a deflating vision, seeing some pretty young girl with her whole life ahead of her, trailing through the airport behind a middle-aged man. OK, I'm aware that sounds like a sweeping generalization but, being totally honest, that's how it seemed to me. All of us at HCU felt so sorry for these girls because they didn't seem to be at all prepared for life in the UK. And perhaps it wasn't what either party might have dreamed of but, maybe in time, these couples did grow to love and care for one another; I dearly hoped so.

The truth was, marriages between UK men and Thai women were on the up. In fact, a little bit of research told me that Thai women preferred British men to any other foreign nationality. The UK was now the most popular foreign source of husbands for young Thai women, who were often seeking a way out of poverty or debasing jobs or were simply looking to broaden their cultural experience.

In the UK, TB is mainly something seen perhaps in the homeless or drug users living rough or in squats, but quite a significant number of these young women from Thailand who'd been granted permanent residency tested positive, which could be seen as a barometer of the country's public health and levels of deprivation. I suppose any woman who agrees to marry a much older man, just to get out of her country for a better life, is not going to be wealthy and educated, so I saw a fair number of women who had nasty, rip-roaring TB. It was on these occasions when problems and dramas often occurred, because TB just wasn't something for which their new husbands were prepared.

# flight risk

Before reaching the UK border, any man bringing back a new wife from Thailand has already been through a fair bit of preparation and groundwork, and it's no walk in the park. The prospective groom has to go the British Embassy in Bangkok to apply for a visa for his bride, probably not realising that only about 5 per cent of applications are accepted. Officials at the embassy rarely believe that they are looking at a genuine marriage, so these guys are knocked back right off the bat.

Jane arrived on the scene, ready to take Prija for her X-ray, but before we could do that it was time for a round of charades, with my amateur and fairly scant acting skills coming into play. This started off with Jane and I dancing around the room, miming 'big bellies' and cradling babes in arms.

'Is there any possibility that you might be pregnant?' Jane said, over-pronouncing to high heaven.

The husband didn't seem to think so but then again I hadn't been particularly encouraged at the flimsy amount of knowledge he had about his new wife, so asking her seemed like a safer bet all round.

The one word she did seem to understand was tuberculosis, with it being fairly universal. In fact, the mere mention of the word prompted a look of defiance from her, coupled with a vigorous shaking of the head.

'No. Of course not. NO!'

Her dark eyes darted around until they came to rest on Jane, waiting to escort her to the X-ray machine. Now she looked terrified. Mr Laurie wasn't looking quite as confident now either, finally caving in and admitting that Prija had been suffering from a cough recently. Jane took her off and did the X-ray, which, when it came back showed that Prija had fairly advanced pulmonary TB.

'I have checked your X-ray and I'm sorry to tell you, but you do have tuberculosis,' I said, pointing at my chest. 'We need to get you some medicine.' Medicine was another word most people understood.

She began to cry and I felt terrible. It was enough that she was with a strange man in a strange country, now some doctor she could barely understand had told her she had a serious illness.

More charades followed as I began pointing and coughing at the poor, frightened girl.

'You. Coughing? A lot?' I coughed violently again, just to hammer the point home. 'Yes?'

Prija shook her head and said, 'I am not coughing,' and then she coughed.

After that, I charade-acted my way through a bunch of other relevant questions: had she been unwell? Was she on medication? Had she been checked for TB in Thailand? The answer to this last question was invariably no, so then I turned to the husband who, by now, was wriggling uncomfortably in his seat.

'Has your wife had any night sweats, Mr Laurie?' I asked and he shrugged.

'Has she lost any weight recently?'

The truth of the matter was that she was so petite, like many of these exquisite brides, I doubt if he'd have been able to even tell whether she'd lost any weight. Again, he didn't seem to have much of an inkling, which made me wonder how well these two people did actually know one another, despite the fact that they'd already tied the knot.

'That's ridiculous,' he said, angry-eyed. 'Surely I'd have known if there was something the matter with her.'

'Mr Laurie, I know it's a shock but I can assure you I'm not mistaken,' I countered. 'It is clear from your wife's X-ray.'

Prija tearfully glanced at her husband. Was I imagining it or was he visibly shrinking away from her as if he might suddenly become infected at that very second? I watched his expression shift from anger to bewilderment as he realized this was a real problem. His pristine bride was faulty goods, suffering from what was essentially a Victorian slum disease. The look on his face was so transparent I had to subdue the sudden burst of anger I felt towards him as I continued.

'Mr Laurie, do you have any symptoms: cough, fever, anything of that nature?'

'What do you mean?' he said.

'Well, TB is quite infectious and I imagine the two of you have spent some time together in close proximity.' I was being as tactful as I could be. 'So if there is anything . . . have you lost any weight, for instance? Any night sweats?'

'No. I haven't,' he said, his voice cold and flat.

He looked like he was about to implode, but when he turned to his wife I caught the look in his eyes. It was as if he was seeing her for the first time: as a real person and not just some fantasy or some shimmering trinket he'd brought home from an exotic holiday. I could almost see the cogs in his brain whirring, wondering what an earth he was going to do next.

Prija, meanwhile, was looking to him for some sort of comfort. With that not forthcoming, I decided to jump in with the good news.

'Look, this is all treatable, even though it's not particularly easy, Mr Laurie. Your wife will need to be on medication, probably for about six months, but it should be curable and she'll be fine.'

'What happens now?' he asked. 'Can we go home?'

'You'll be issued with a Port 103 document, which is a legal document that requires you, first thing tomorrow, to phone the local consultant for Communicable Disease Control,' I told him. 'That department will then enable your wife to get urgent medical treatment for her TB. It's a condition of entry into the country that you contact them straight away. So we will in turn contact the department and tell them to expect your call. Do you think you can explain all that to your wife?'

Mr Laurie nodded but appeared dazed. 'I just need to go and collect something from outside,' he said.

He jumped out of his chair as if it was on fire, and as he turned his back and headed towards the door, it flashed through my mind that this man just might just do a runner and leave his sick wife stranded at the airport. There was something about his demeanour; the way his whole attitude had changed the second he found out she was infected. Some of the men I'd met under similar circumstances had been caring and supportive, eager to get their new brides all the help they needed, but there was something different about this one. This clearly wasn't what he'd signed up for at all and I felt that I had to say something.

'Just a second, Mr Laurie.' He froze and turned around, eyes wide. 'I just want to make it clear that your wife needs looking after during all this. She's had bad news and she's in a strange country, and it's your responsibility to make sure she gets the help and the medication she needs. You do understand that, don't you?'

'Of course.' He barely opened his mouth as he spoke, so I tried to reassure him.

'If there is any way that you have also been infected, you'll get all the help you need too. It's not something that is fatal in the UK; it's a completely treatable and curable condition.'

The fact is we're very lucky in the UK because treatment is free. If you're unlucky enough to catch TB, then it will be sorted.

The man made a swift exit out of the room, and I wondered if that might be the last either she or I saw of him. Once he was gone, a look of dread crept over the young woman's face, so I smiled confidently back at her.

'You're going to be all right,' I said, gently.

Perhaps she was thinking the same thing that I was; that her brand-new spouse was legging it through Terminal 3 as fast as his feet would carry him at this very moment. I hoped I was wrong.

I completed the relevant paperwork for Prija's ongoing treatment, while she sat in the cubicle, quietly coming to terms with her predicament. Just as I was finishing up, Mr Laurie reappeared at the door.

'Oh, you're back!' I was surprised at how relieved I felt to see him.

A weak smile crossed his lips. 'Of course I am,' he said, as if my astonishment was evident.

I handed him a letter. 'Well, everything has been arranged. This will explain exactly what you need to do next.'

'Thank you, Doctor,' he said. 'I'll make sure she gets the

help. I'm sorry if I was a little . . . you know . . . it's just that . . .'

'That's perfectly all right, Mr Laurie,' I said with a smile. 'I just hope everything works out for you both.' I looked across at Prija. 'And you *will* be all right. Trust me.'

Mr Laurie put the letter into his pocket and turned to his wife, who was looking up at him anxiously.

'Shall we go, Prija?' He held out his hand to her and she finally smiled.

Mandy, Jane and I watched Prija and her new husband walk out of HCU, hand in hand, Prija looking back at us nervously, just before she disappeared out into her new world.

'It does make me wonder what sort of life she must have had,' Mandy said.

'You mean for her to marry a man she hardly knew and move halfway across the world? I *always* wonder that,' Jane said.

Mandy nodded. 'She was a really pretty girl.'

'Most of them are,' I said.

By then, I'd seen Thai brides of all different varieties coming through HCU: shy, optimistic, bewildered, and even a couple who appeared to have their new husbands wrapped around their little fingers, but more often that not they were just nervous young women, credulous and disadvantaged in an alien environment.

Going about the rest of my day, I considered what might happen to Prija and Mr Laurie down the line. How long could a relationship last, built on such flimsy foundations? Him being so much older and neither of them speaking the same language? He having married someone he barely knew because he was lonely and she marrying him because she needed an escape route from a hard life. I consoled myself with the reminder that at least he'd come back for her, and *had promised* to get her the medical help she needed. For now, that would have to be good enough.

## 13

# asylum

THE GEOPOLITICS OF THE AIRPORT were fascinating, with the state of the world directly influencing the nationality of the passengers who passed through HCU. Obviously the most direct effect of world events was on those claiming political asylum (called PAs). When I started at Heathrow in 2001, the majority of PAs were families from Poland and Romania, and it was clear to me that most were economic migrants. Once those countries joined the European Union, we no longer saw them in HCU as they could enter the UK freely and without any checks. Then after 9/11 and the war in Afghanistan, PAs came predominantly from Afghanistan and Iraq. For a while we had Zimbabweans claiming asylum; this time it was the white farmers who were being persecuted by Mugabe and having their land confiscated. It was just another ethnic group, but an interesting contrast. And latterly, of course, we saw Syrian PAs. The homelands and motivations of asylum seekers changed as the geopolitical scenario did.

There are many reasons why people arrive at Heathrow seeking a safe haven in the UK, but, as I learned quite swiftly, all petitions are not equal and therefore not all are successful. During my time I saw many people who really were desperate to get out of the situation they'd found themselves in back in their home country, and clearly deserving of asylum. But the IOs also encountered people who they suspected did not have a legitimate claim, and it was often those cases, particularly where people had gone to extraordinary lengths to get here, that I was called to act upon.

It would often be when I was just sitting down for a rest that a call would come through telling me that someone had collapsed in the immigration hall. On one particular day, it was Jack on the other end of the line, telling me about a woman arriving from a flight from Kenya who had collapsed just as he was questioning her about the validity of her visa. This looked decidedly iffy. It wasn't unusual for people to collapse at this very moment, in fact the immigration hall and passport control were fairly common places for a seizure, fainting spell or even a heart attack, and most of the ones I attended there turned out to be bogus. The recurring idea behind this ruse is that the 'patient' will be ambulanced off to hospital, and from there he or she can do a runner. In these cases, it's usually the timing of the 'seizure' that's a dead giveaway, but it's often coupled with some of the most criminally bad acting I've ever seen. Nevertheless, I always dashed to attend.

On hearing the rather suspect timing of this woman's apparent collapse, my instinct was that this was one of those cases. This middle-aged lady, having flown in from Kenya, had by all accounts been perfectly robust all the way over here, right up until the officer started grilling her over her suspect document. That said, I couldn't afford to be complacent about a patient's wellbeing – you just never knew – so I got to the immigration hall as quickly as I could, armed with my oxygen. We don't keep a crash cart at HCU, that's just something the paramedics have. The trouble is, the paramedics are always miles away when you need them, so I'm always the first port of call and I just have to do what I can until the paramedics get there if needed.

When I arrived in the hall, Jack filled me in on what had happened.

'I told her that the visa in her passport didn't look right and the next thing she was clutching her chest. Then she just crumpled and fell on the floor.'

'OK, let me have a look at her,' I said, heading towards

the large woman who, I must say, did look like she was in considerable pain.

Maybe I was wrong. Maybe this woman had had a heart attack. Kneeling down beside her, I asked if she could hear me and readied myself to start my basic life-support check: airways, breathing, circulation, and so on. Hang on, though. One minute she was clutching the right side of her chest, and the next it was the left side.

'Are you having trouble breathing?' I asked.

The woman nodded, writhing around on the airport floor with her eyes shut tight. I reminded myself of the first time something like this happened, in my first few days at HCU, I'd been quite alarmed with the urgency and panic of it all, especially in the midst of a busy airport with people bustling around the scene. I was stunned when it turned out that the guy whose life I was desperately trying to save turned out to be a chancer with a fake passport. By now I was a little more wise to this sort of scam. Of course I still had to go through the motions, just to be sure, but I could usually get a feel for one of these hackneyed scenarios pretty swiftly.

'I'm the airport doctor,' I told the woman. 'If you can get up, I'll take you to my room and I can check you over and see what the problem is.'

She glanced up at me, all trace of her horrendous pain subsiding momentarily. Then she shook her head.

'Look, I can't examine you here because we're in the middle of the immigration hall, but if you can just come to my room I can check you over. Then I can call an ambulance and get you to hospital.'

The woman looked up at me again but this time I got up and walked away, back towards HCU. I counted to five and then looked behind me, and sure enough there she was, trotting along behind me, pulling her little wheelie carry-on bag behind her.

Once she was in HCU, she buckled again and fell back on to the examination couch. This time she looked, quite convincingly, like she was out cold. Sinead was on the front desk and looked concerned.

'What's the matter with her?' she said.

'I'm not sure there's anything the matter with her,' I whispered.

'So I'll not bother calling the paramedics then?'

Sinead was a sharp-tongued Irish woman who, I had to admit, scared me slightly; she was meat-and-potatoes no non-sense, and had been there and done it all as far as working at Heathrow was concerned.

'I'd better just make sure,' I said.

There was a way we had checking for pain, where you dug your fingernail into the patient's nail-bed. You're not allowed to do it any more because it's considered too painful – nowadays you'd press the sternum or squeeze the trapezius, which is one of the major muscles of the upper back, to check for pain, but that's what we did back then, and if the patient felt the pain of it, they'd withdraw or wake up or whatever. She winced when I did it, but then just slipped back into 'unconsciousness'. Within seconds, Albert, one of the airport's team of paramedics, was on the scene.

'One of the IOs called to say you might need us,' he said, enthusiastically.

Albert was one of several Heathrow staff who were currently involved in a fly-on-the-wall documentary about the airport, so he often had camera and sound people running around after him, and today was no exception.

'Do they all have to be in here?' Sinead said, as Albert moved towards the woman.

I looked up to see a man with a camera, a young woman with a pad and pen, and a nervous-looking lad with a clapperboard.

'It's just the show,' Albert said, like it was an everyday thing having a camera crew trailing around after you.

'Is this what you call entertainment?' Sinead asked – she was never one to mince words.

'No, I'm sorry, I don't think they can be in here right now,' I said. 'Albert, you're going to have to do this sans the glare of the spotlight I'm afraid. We need to get this lady checked over. They can come back in a minute.'

The production team, who were fast becoming a permanent fixture at Heathrow, followed Sinead's finger, backing out of the room, while Albert loomed over the woman who, by this time, had opened her eyes.

'Are you having trouble breathing?' he said, and the woman nodded, gasping with renewed vitality.

'We are not convinced,' Sinead said, rather too loudly, and Albert looked back at her, raising his eyebrows in confirmation.

'Are you feeling dizzy?' Albert said, as if the woman were a five-year-old.

She nodded.

'And are you seeing little triangles in front of your eyes?'

'Yes, I'm seeing triangles,' the woman said.

I could hear Sinead chuckling behind me. This was one of Albert's stock questions to people he believed to be faking collapse. Triangles instead of stars. It never failed to amuse.

In the end, Albert and I saw no reason why the woman needed to be taken to hospital so I took her blood pressure and listened to her chest – a pretty cursory examination as I was now fairly convinced there was nothing wrong with her – then I checked her temperature, which was normal. I think by that point even she'd got bored with the charade as she was now sitting up and looking at a text on her phone.

Back outside HCU I found Jack, who'd been waiting for news of the woman's condition.

'She's fine, Jack, miraculous recovery,' I said. 'You can carry on questioning her.'

Jack grinned at me. 'Thank you, Dr Green.'

One of the asylum cases that raised some questions for me involved a Columbian woman who came in for a quick health check as was our practice with all PAs. When Mandy and I entered the cubicle to examine her, she was sitting on a chair, serene and calm with her eyes softly closed, as if she were meditating.

'Do you speak any English?' I asked.

Her eyes opened like shutters and she took me in. 'What's going to happen to me?'

Yes, she spoke English.

'Well, I'm going to check you over quickly and then we're going to give you an X-ray, is that all right?'

'I'll do whatever you want.' Her voice was shaky; all traces of serenity gone.

'It's nothing to worry about, honestly,' I said.

She managed a half-smile as I approached her, noting how nattily dressed she was, with coiffured hair and glamorous make-up. I'd have guessed she was in her mid-thirties.

'Are you all right?' I asked. 'Are you worried about something?' Her smoky eyes darted up to meet mine, but she didn't speak. 'It's OK, you don't have to answer.'

I could feel her heart thumping as I listened to her chest and I wondered what this woman's story was. When I'd finished looking her over, she puffed out a sigh of relief.

'Terrible things in my country.' She shook her head. 'I had to flee for my life, taking nothing. I just had to run. Run with only the things I could carry.'

'That's awful, but why?' I said. 'What did you do to put yourself in such danger?'

'I did nothing, but I think I probably would have been killed if I had stayed even an hour longer,' she said. 'I'm sure of it.'

I listened, nodding empathetically as she unfurled a heart-rending story, full of desperation and peril. Then I looked down and clocked the rollerblades poking out of the top of her Louis Vuitton bag.

I'm sorry, rollerblades?

Call me cynical, but might this woman's story have been embellished somewhat here and there?

'Well, thank goodness you had time to grab your roller-blades while you were fleeing for your life,' I thought to myself. We've all heard the phrase 'get your skates on' when someone is in a desperate rush, but she'd clearly taken the phrase quite literally.

'Let's just get that X-ray done, shall we?' I said quickly, trying and failing to shoo away the vision of her rollerblading through the streets of Bogotá with government assassins in hot pursuit.

Perhaps she had a good enough reason for wanting to come and live in the UK, but unless she'd had time to cram in a shopping trip and full makeover before getting on the plane, fleeing for her life with mere seconds to spare wasn't it. It was more than possible that she had a valid claim for asylum but over-egging her story like that was not going to help her case. I couldn't help thinking about the men and women who actually *were* fleeing for their lives from various war-torn countries and, although I couldn't be sure, her case stood in stark contrast to the cases of very real plight that we encountered at HCU.

It reminded me of a story that an IO had told me when I first started working at Heathrow, about a group of twenty-five people from Afghanistan who had landed at Terminal 4, all claiming asylum. He said there was something unusual about this well-turned-out party of men and women, not least the fact that they'd chartered their own private jet and reserved a landing slot at the airport, all of which costs vast amounts of money. This surprised me at the time, as I'd always imagined that asylum seekers could barely afford to get to the UK, but these people looked well off and had, it turned out, paid various agents and organizations a fair amount of dosh to help them charter the plane and co-ordinate their arrival at Heathrow. Of course it was quite possible that they were political refugees of some kind, but given there had been an entire jet-load of them, it did make me wonder.

Even for people who aren't seeking asylum, the UK is often seen as a beacon of hope and opportunity by those from countries whose social care isn't as good as ours. I once encountered a man from Pakistan, who had come because he needed a triple bypass and felt the doctors in the UK would do a better job than in his own country. I recall another man telling me that he had been told that Tony Blair would give him a house if he came to the UK and had literally jumped on a plane with his family. As he entered HCU, he told me this as if he expected me to hand him the keys there and then.

This belief that British doctors will be on hand to solve their health problems as soon as they arrive in the UK can lead to people taking dreadful risks when they're travelling.

One day, when I'd been at Heathrow long enough to think I could no longer be surprised, a Bangledeshi woman was brought to HCU because she had reported feeling unwell as she was coming through the immigration hall. When I spoke to her, she told me she had renal failure and she was on dialysis every three days, and her dialysis was due that day.

'You mean you need treatment straight away?' I said.

The woman nodded at me as if she'd been asking for an extra

carrier bag at Sainsbury's rather than vital therapy required to keep her alive.

'Well, have you arranged this? Is there anything in place for the rest of your visit?' I asked, somewhat agog.

The woman shook her head. 'Could you do it for me here?'

'Oddly enough, we don't have a dialysis machine at the airport, so I'm afraid not,' I said.

It seemed incredible to me that somebody would make a trip to a country thousands of miles away without making prior arrangements for a treatment they essentially couldn't live without. She'd arranged a visa to come, there was nothing wrong with her mentally, but there had been no advance preparation for her lifesaving therapy. She'd just flown in, taking it for granted that somebody would magically organize kidney dialysis on her arrival.

I spent the next hour scrabbling around, trying to sort something out. In the end, the renal team at Hillingdon Hospital agreed to take her, although they were fit to bursting at the time of my call. The paramedics transported the woman that evening to the hospital, where she would receive her dialysis that night or the next morning. Good old Hillingdon. As the local and therefore go-to hospital for a huge, international airport like Heathrow, they had a tough time: expected to deal with everything and anyone needing hospitalization or treatment other than that which we could give at the airport, as well as their own patients. And this was no small amount of spillover either. In fact, Heathrow generated so much extra work for Hillingdon that they ultimately had to apply for extra funding from the government to cope with the financial impact.

On a busy evening at HCU, I might be scrutinizing X-rays of people with suspected TB, checking for pregnancy and attending to a person who'd become ill during a flight. Late one evening I was finishing looking at the day's X-rays when an IO brought in a young man who had been in their holding room all day.

While Customs held drug mules in their cells, anyone else who'd been held back, for whatever reason, was put in the holding rooms until after the last flight had arrived when there would be time to question and process them fully. I never had cause to see the cells at Heathrow, but the holding rooms were just depressing little spaces with a vending machine and a few plastic chairs. Most people wouldn't even notice them going through the airport, but they were situated on the far left-hand side of the immigration hall, just past where you show your passport as you come through – adjacent to HCU. These rooms were presided over by security guards who were separated from the detainees by a glass office, so they could keep an eye on the unfortunates awaiting their fate without actually mixing with them. This zoo-like atmosphere was one of the reasons I disliked going into the holding rooms and why I never wanted families with young children to be held in them, especially as there could be other detainees in there too. Fortunately this is no longer allowed.

'Do you think this boy is under eighteen, Doctor? He's not got any papers and there's nothing to prove his age.'

It wasn't unusual for me to be asked to speculate on someone's age who was wanting to enter the country as a minor, but I wasn't a fan of this kind of enquiry. The truth is, it's quite hard to prove somebody's age; in fact there is no definitive way. Remember when the migrant and refugee camp in Calais, known as the 'Jungle', shut down in 2016? The UK pledged to take unaccompanied minors under its care, but some of the 'minors' who came through looked more as if they were in their mid-twenties, and there was an outcry in certain quarters.

There are various practical investigations which can be undertaken to help determine age: for example, looking at wisdom teeth or X-raying the hands to ascertain bone age. But people are not trees and, as I said, there really is no definitive way. And anyway, at Heathrow we were only allowed to perform chest X-rays, which ruled out X-raying hands, so that theory wouldn't have been much use to anyone. Because there was no way to be sure, we weren't officially supposed to speculate although if I looked at an individual and was confident that they were over eighteen, then I might say so. But officially the HCU line was 'we don't assess age'.

Having agreed with the IO that this young man did indeed appear to be over eighteen, I turned back to the X-rays. Five minutes later the same IO returned with a second individual claiming asylum. This man had told Immigration that he was an activist who didn't want to hurt innocent people, but that his life was in danger as he was considered a terrorist in his home country. He was claiming asylum, professing he'd been tortured by his own government, so Immigration wanted me to examine him for evidence of that torture. The thing was, this small man with sad eyes and scrawny arms was the antithesis of how one might imagine an enemy of the state to look: gentle, quiet and unthreatening. As he undressed to his underwear for the examination, he stared around the cubicle warily, rather like a cornered animal.

'Can you tell me what you told Immigration about the nature of your torture?' I asked.

He nodded slowly, looking as though he only half understood what I was saying.

'They mentioned you'd been shot, is that correct?'

'Yes, I was shot,' he said, and pointed to the upper right side of his chest.

I could see a short, wide scar, but I couldn't be sure whether it was a historic bullet wound or not. On his back I noticed some other marks; small coins of shrivelled skin, and quite a few of them.

'What about these marks?' I said, feeling one of them gently. 'What caused this?'

The man tapped two fingers to his lips and at first I couldn't fathom what he was trying to say.

'Cigarette,' he said. He mimed stubbing a cigarette out on his own neck. 'They put cigarettes on me. I never hurt anybody.'

I checked again; these marks certainly looked like cigarette burns. I wondered what an X-ray might throw up and called Jane to take him in.

'What exactly happened to you?' I asked.

'I was captive of government,' he said. 'I was shot and taken. I was shot here too.'

He gestured towards his leg, matter-of factly. Whatever was there looked as though it was healed, but there was a fair-sized chunk missing from his calf so that part of his story certainly added up.

'So how long were you held in prison for?' I said.

The man shook his head. 'Not in prison so much. Detained. Torture. They beat me. Tried to make me tell them about our activities.'

He spoke like he was telling me about a pleasant day out in the park, rather than government-sponsored torture, so I nodded, not feeling that I could ask him any more because he'd already been interviewed by Immigration and no doubt would be again. It didn't really matter what the background story was to me anyway. My responsibility was to determine whether the physical manifestations were consistent with the PA's account of what had happened.

A couple of minutes later, Jane came in and we took him through to be X-rayed. She and I looked at the results together while he waited back in the cubicle.

'Look at this,' Jane said. She was pointing at tiny white flecks, clearly visible in his chest.

'I think it's pieces of shot,' I said. 'He told me this is where he was shot.'

'So you think it's true he was tortured?'

'Obviously I can't be 100 per cent, but there is evidence of injury,' I said. 'He certainly has wounds that are consistent with his story, so that's what I'm going to tell Immigration.'

Having heard the man's story, I hoped that my assessment would help. I knew whatever happened next, it was going to be a lengthy legal process for him, but I found myself hoping that he would eventually be granted asylum. Why? Because he looked like a man who didn't want to fight any more.

# 14

# the fugitive

ON A TWENTY-FOUR-HOUR SHIFT, a typical day meant I'd start at 10am, taking over from one of the doctors in Terminal 4, who'd been there overnight. Then, unless I was called to an incident aboard a plane or to another terminal, I'd spend the day working in Terminal 4 up until 6.30pm, when I'd drive over to Terminal 3 to take over from the doctor who'd been working there from seven in the morning on a twelve-hour shift.

Terminal 4 was pretty quiet in the evening, so it was just staffed by HCOs. From seven in the evening, the doctor on a twenty-four hour shift would base themselves at Terminal 3 because that was where all the action was, with a huge number of flights coming in. Most people tend to travel on their national airline, usually the most affordable option, and almost all the non-BA long-haul flights came in to Terminal 3. Those from less economically developed countries such as Nigeria, Bangladesh, Pakistan and India always generated the most work for us with students, long-stay visitors and those with work visas just some of the people we'd have to X-ray or examine.

At about 11pm, I'd see anyone who was still in the holding room as quickly as possible before heading back over to my sleeping quarters at Terminal 4, which is where the all-powerful DO came in. Cindy, who had bright red hair, was an extremely energetic personality and one of the DOs whom I really liked. She showed those dogs that look a bit like a floor mop (the kind with grey dreadlocks – I think they were Bergamascos), spending much of her leisure time at Cruft's and other dog shows, showing her prize-winning pets, who were her life. She was always my favourite DO to work with because she was so efficient and got things done. Come 11 o'clock on an evening shift in Terminal 3 when Cindy was on duty, she'd be out there, hassling the Chief IO to send us any asylum seekers – or anyone else who needed to go through HCU – as quickly as possible.

'The doctor wants to head over to Terminal 4 and get her head down,' she'd bark, sending all the IOs rushing around to get things sorted rather than incurring her wrath. She was always dynamic, and usually quite fun too.

# the fugitive

On one reasonably quiet summer's evening in Terminal 3, things were winding down and my mind was already drifting to thoughts of my less than comfortable bed. Luxurious or not, I was tired and it was time to rest. It was always easier to get off to sleep when things hadn't been frantic with my mind going nineteen to the dozen, reliving all that had happened in the previous few hours. So with no more flights due to come in and Cindy giving me the all clear, I was hopeful of some restful, if not completely undisturbed, shut-eye. I was just about to head over to Terminal 4 when I heard shouting, followed by what sounded like a crash. I'd barely had time to register the commotion before I heard a flustered voice yelling from outside the office.

'Dr Green, are you there? Could you come with us, quick as you can, please?'

Propelled out of my chair, I called back, 'I'll be right out!'

Outside, I was greeted by Tom, whose eyes were full of panic.

'One of the detainees has kicked off big time,' he said. 'I think he's going to need serious medical assistance.'

'Kicked off how?' I wondered if this might be some kind of violent physical attack I was about to attend.

'He picked up a bin – one of the big freestanding ones – and smashed it through the window of the holding room,' Tom said. 'Then after the bin went out of the window, he threw himself out after it.'

'What?'

I pictured the windows in the holding room, the glass of which was completely blacked out. Could the guy have even known what he was jumping into? Or been aware of the fact that the room was three storeys up?

'OK, let me get my things and I'll be right there,' I said.

Gathering up my kit, I followed Tom out of HCU who explained to me that the 'jumper' had earlier been found hiding in one of the toilets trying to flush away his passport before he got to Immigration. This was something people did so their nationality would be hard to pinpoint and they could be less than truthful about where they'd come from and claim asylum – which was far more likely to be granted if they were fleeing from a war zone or a country where they might be persecuted. Some of them had already flushed their passports down the toilets of the plane, having been told to do so by the facilitators of their attempted escape. As you might imagine, the people flushing their passports down the plane loos were quite often *not* the ones from danger zones, hence the need for deception. There were certain airlines on certain routes that had constantly blocked toilet systems due to the shredding and attempted disposal of passports.

Once they'd arrived, people with something to hide often tried secreting themselves in the toilets, or somewhere that seemed to offer some cover. If they weren't trying to flush

the fugitive

away their passports, they could be simply staying out of sight,
planning to sneak through when the coast was clear, in the
early hours of the morning. For this reason, every night, once
the last plane had landed, airport security carried out what's
known as 'the sweep'. This entailed a full search of the building
for any potential asylum seekers or smugglers who might be
hiding in a toilet or a cupboard, somewhere in the no-man's-
land that lies between the plane and Border Control. It wasn't
unusual for them to find somebody – people trying their luck
at hiding in the airport is a more common occurrence than
you'd imagine.

Anybody found during the sweep was brought to HCU,
and there we would examine and X-ray them for TB. Of
course, many of those claiming political asylum were genuinely
desperate and would have done pretty much anything to gain
entry into the UK by whatever means possible.

During the sweep on this particular night, the man had been
caught mid-flush, and escorted to a room next to HCU where
he was detained and watched over by the security guards. He
wasn't the only person in the holding room at the time. There
were always a few detainees left over from earlier whose destiny
and indeed destination were yet to be decided. Some might
have had suspect passports, and there may have been concerns
about others coming into the country at all. By all accounts,
our man had been a bit more twitchy than most, and while

the duty security guard was distracted for a second, filling in some paperwork, the jumper took his chances.

The futility of our dash into the holding room didn't hit me until we reached the door. The man had already jumped out of the window so was of course not there. There was no point us being there either. Still, it was quite a scene, with the other detainees looking just as shocked as the guards. It was evident this had been a fairly crazed and violent attack on the window: the glass was thick and hard to penetrate, so the guy had come at it with considerable force. I walked across the room and peered tentatively out of the smashed window. Nothing.

'Can you see him?' Tom asked.

I looked down and shook my head. 'I can't see anyone. We'd best go down.'

Without even thinking about it and with no real idea where I was going, I ran out of the room with Tom and a pair of security guards trundling along behind me. The route to the spot outside where the man would have fallen was quite convoluted, but I knew the area well as it was where all the baggage cars from Terminal 3 went to be unloaded, and also where I and the other doctors parked our cars. By the time we got down there, a couple of unarmed police officers had come to help with the search, as the guy was obviously desperate and potentially dangerous. I assumed he must have injured himself during such a fall, so I had Tom call an ambulance too. When we reached the spot where our jumper would have dropped, however, he was nowhere to be seen. There was shattered glass and there was a crushed bin, but no fugitive detainee anywhere to be found.

'Well, he can't be all that injured,' I said to one of the guards, who shook his head.

'He also can't be too far away, Doctor,' he said.

It was pitch black by then so this wasn't going to be the easiest, or safest, of tasks, but we had to find him fast. He may have been sick, he might have been hurt. Before I knew it, I was wandering around the nooks and crannies of a dark, deserted, late-night airport, searching for a man who had been desperate enough to smash his way out of a plate-glass window, three floors up. It didn't take a genius to work out that he wasn't going to give up easily and would do anything to avoid recapture.

For a while I stalked around with Tom and one of the security guards, peeking under cars and around dormant baggage trucks, but pretty soon I was on my own, quietly enjoying the drama of the situation and hoping that I'd be the one to find him, especially as I was more familiar with this corner of the airport than the others.

'Any luck?' I heard somebody call out, followed by a chorus of 'No' and 'Not yet'.

I was just covering a particularly deserted corner of the car park when my phone rang and scared the shit out of me. It was Chris, who always called me when I was on the nightshift, just before he was heading off to bed.

'Jesus Christ!' I said, answering.

'No, it's just me,' Chris said. 'Just phoning to say have a good night and I'll see you tomorrow. You busy there, or is it nice and quiet this evening?'

'Well, funny you should say that,' I said. 'I'm actually wandering around in the dark looking for an escaped detainee.'

Chris was silent for a moment before saying, 'Oh, really?'

'I'm searching a car park for a man who smashed through the window of the holding room and escaped,' I clarified. 'It's actually quite exciting.'

'It's what?'

'Well, at least it's broken up the day a bit,' I said.

I tend to have scant regard for my own safety. It's not that I'm physically brave; I think it's just a case of having a practical approach and getting on with the job in hand. Plus I honestly believe that when you're a doctor you just don't think about it that much. Chris, on the other hand, wasn't quite so blasé about the idea of me hunting down a potentially dangerous absconder in the dead of night.

'But there's someone with you, isn't there? You're not doing this on your own?'

'Don't be daft, darling,' I said.

I looked over my shoulder and realized that there wasn't in fact anybody else in close proximity. In the distance I could see a few heads bobbing up and down in between parked cars, but that was about it. We needed to check the car park, all the offices down there and the transfer bus station too, so by then we'd all very much spread out to cover as much ground as we could. With baggage trolleys and all sorts of things around, there were a lot of potential hiding places.

'Well, there are other people involved in the search,' I said, peeking behind a group of large metal bins.

'But are they right there with you, is what I'm asking,' Chris said.

'Not exactly,' I said. Chris fell silent for a few seconds. 'Chris, are you still there?'

'Steph, I really don't think you should be doing this.' His voice was even, but I could hear the underlying urgency. 'I think this is something you should leave to the police and the airport security.'

'Well yes, but the guy might be injured so . . .'

'That's not the point,' Chris said. 'What I'm saying is, maybe you should just go and sit in your car until they find him and then if they need you, they can call you.'

'Yes, I suppose that would be more sensible,' I said, knowing full well I had absolutely no intention of sitting in the car and missing all the excitement.

'Just be careful, Steph. Please.'

'Darling, nothing is going to happen to me. I'm with lots of other people and besides that, the guy we're searching for has gone and jumped through a bloody window three storeys up, so I'd imagine he's going to be quite injured. I'm not going to do anything silly, trust me.'

This was an odd turnaround for us. In contrast to my constant stressing about stuff, Chris is generally calm and phlegmatic.

I am always amazed by how kind and extremely patient he is with the seemingly endless parade of highly strung staff who've worked in his pubs and hotels over the years. There always seems to be a drama with one of them, and Chris will listen attentively before giving them a pep talk and sending them on their way – he's brilliant at managing a team. I think this is also because he's one of those people who tends to see the best in others, which is also in contrast to me, as I seem to be unable to suffer fools and am a tad more cynical than he is. Like Jane Austen's Mr Darcy: *My good opinion once lost is lost forever.'*

The strange thing about that night was, if Chris hadn't voiced his concern regarding my safety, I don't think it would have even entered my mind. I was just in the moment, getting on with the job and that was all there was to it. The fact that I was running around in the dark searching for someone who might have appeared from the shadows and attacked me at any time didn't really come into it. The truth of it was actually so serious that a few more minutes into our search, the rag-tag search party of me, Tom and a few security guards was bolstered with an array of big macho guys with machine guns and dogs – the armed police officers. Now things were really getting serious. So, after I'd hung up the phone with Chris, promising to be extra vigilant, I made sure I stayed closer to the other searchers.

The longer the man was loose, the bigger and more intense the search party seemed to get, but now it was the domain of the armed police, who very much took the lead. This elite group was a different breed to the rest of us at the airport, or at least that's how they came across, and they certainly pulled rank over the other police and security staff. One has to be a certain type of person to be firearms trained: you have to be prepared to take the shots and to put yourself in danger, and when it comes down to it, these were the men and women who were trained to run towards the suspected terrorists rather than away from them. They always had an assertive air, with their bulletproof vests and their walkie-talkies and handcuffs dangling off their belts. In fact, they carried such an impressive amount of kit I wondered whether they would be able to make a dash for it if required. My only complaint was that some of the men had a real air of superiority and could be quite dismissive of the rest of us. I'm quite intolerant of that.

On the other hand, some of them had fantastically gorgeous Alsatian dogs, and being a real dog-lover meant I was always drawn to them like a spoon to a magnet. And yes, I know you're not really supposed to pet working dogs when they're on the job, but they were just so magnificent . . . Consequently, I was always getting stern looks from the dog handlers and even, on occasion, shouted at.

'STAND BACK FROM THE DOG. IT IS NOT A PET!'

Well yes, I know it's not a pet, I'd think, but then again I'm hardly somebody they're being asked to catch or kill, am I? I'm just a nice woman in a white coat who wants to say hello to a beautiful dog. I know they can't be treated as mollycoddled pets, but I didn't see how a pat on the head from a member of staff was going to hamper their performance. I told myself that it was just the armed police's way of retaining that little extra bit of mystique. That was my theory anyway.

The search continued for some time until a call rang out across the car park.

'We've found him!'

'Is Dr Green there?' someone else shouted.

I headed across the car park where our 'dangerous fugitive' had been discovered cowering behind a baggage trolley: not threatening or violent, but scared and confused. Unsurprisingly, he'd been injured – a broken ankle, I thought – so the paramedics were called and he went straight off to hospital with plenty of security in tow. It was a bit of a damp squib after all the excitement, to be honest, but even so it certainly wasn't an everyday occurrence that somebody threw themselves through a third-storey window.

I felt a little deflated after the panic was over. Lying in bed for ages, unable to sleep, I pondered the night's events. What really stuck in my mind was this man's extraordinary desperation: to smash and then jump through a window, into the unknown, risking laceration or even death, and on top of that believing that in a place like Heathrow Airport he'd be able to avoid capture. I wish I'd known what the man's story was and where he was from. What had driven him to such lengths? To dispose of his passport, his very identity, and then to risk his life rather than be told that he couldn't enter the country. I saw desperation during my time in HCU; some of it sad and some bordering on the comic, but this was certainly the most dramatic.

## 15

## sleepless

FOR A SHORT WHILE we couldn't sleep in Terminal 4 due to building work, so we slept in Terminal 5 instead, in what was basically the clinical room. The bed had a waterproof mattress in case of incontinence; it was slippery, uncomfortable and made me sweat. The room had a light that was activated by movement, so whenever I turned over in bed the whole place lit up. Rather illegally, each night I stood on a chair and taped a piece of paper over the sensor so that it would stay dark all night. And it was just as chilly as the room in Terminal 4. You might be wondering why, in all the years I'd worked there, I never brought in a nice 13-tog duvet from home, but I had enough stuff to lug in with me as it was: food, wash bag, nightclothes, change-of clothes, and besides that there was nowhere to store it anyway.

On one of the nights at Terminal 5, I lay in bed considering Dr Crosby's warning that I mustn't stay too long because the job was a dead end. I'd now been at Heathrow for eight years, but that certainly didn't make him right. If anything, he'd done a disservice to the job, not realizing just how fascinating it would turn out to be and how much I'd see and learn. It might not have been on the traditional career path but the experience had been invaluable. We never knew what would come through the doors of HCU next so it had taught me to think on my feet, and despite the distinct lack of glamour in the doctor's sleeping quarters, this job sat well in my life.

That being said, I just couldn't get off to sleep that night. I was over-tired after a taxing day shift that had felt eternal. After an unusually large glut of X-rays that threw up two cases of TB, I'd spent a good part of the evening trying to calm down a young man who'd been bitten by a monkey. Yes, a monkey. I headed into the examination room at about nine o'clock, to be faced with a young man of about twenty-one, his hands shaking like mad.

'Are you the doctor?' he blurted at me. 'I need your help.'

I'd already had notification that this young Irish man was arriving at Heathrow from North Africa, but I wasn't bargaining on him being quite so distraught.

'You're Kevin, is that right?' I asked, as gently as I could.

'Yes, Kevin Walsh,' he said, almost shouting. 'I think I might have caught rabies.'

This was pure panic, the like of which I hadn't seen for a long time.

'And why do you think that, Kevin? Have you had any symptoms?'

'No, but I was bitten by a monkey this morning,' he said.

'So I understand,' I said. 'And after you were bitten did you . . .'

'It was a research trip for my degree,' he cut in. 'I mean, it really took a chunk out of me, the cheeky little bastard.'

I resisted the urge to smile, but as Kevin continued he got more het up, bordering on hysterical: running his hands over his cropped head, his breath coming in short, sharp blasts. It struck me that his reaction was somewhat out of proportion, given that he'd shown no signs of having contracted anything, let alone rabies.

'But you saw a doctor after you were bitten, is that right?'

Kevin nodded. 'Yes, she gave me an injection right where the bite was.'

This first immunoglobulin injection, administered straight into the wound after an animal bite, is a solution of antibodies that essentially mop up any rabies virus that might be there. After that, a person who is potentially exposed but who has never been vaccinated should receive an initial dose of vaccine followed by subsequent doses on the third, seventh and four-teenth days. Kevin had received the antibodies in the local hospital where he'd been treated, and they had then notified us at Port Health that he'd be arriving at Heathrow later in the day to have his first injection and collect more vaccine, which he could then take to his GP to be administered as prescribed. We did keep batches of rabies vaccine at Heathrow, in fact we were one of the few medical facilities who did. One of my main responsibilities as a doctor at Heathrow was to keep nasty infections from coming into the country, and since the UK is completely clear of rabies, we'd almost been stockpiling it at one point. The trouble was we hardly ever used it, so the HCOs were forever checking the dates and throwing it out because it had expired. It just became a waste to keep too much of it at once.

'I'll have a look at the bite and give you an injection now,' I said. 'How did it happen anyway? Were you handling it?'

'Not exactly,' he said. 'We were up in the hills on a field study. We'd stopped to have a bite to eat and . . . well, I sup-pose it was after the food I had in my hand. It just sort of sneaked down a tree and the next thing it was leaning over me. I put my arm out to push it away and that was it. My so-called friends thought it was hysterical, me with a bloody monkey hanging off my arm, but it really hurt. And it took my fucking sandwich.'

He almost broke into a smile, but it was fleeting. Instead, Kevin rolled up his sleeve and looked at me, wincing as I gave him the first dose of vaccine into his deltoid muscle. After that, I talked him through his upcoming regimen of treatment, but he wasn't at all convinced that it was going to be enough.

'Well, there must be something else I need, apart from injections. Other treatments?' he said.

'This is honestly sufficient,' I assured him. 'I'll be giving you vaccine for your next dose, which you can then take to your GP and . . .'

Kevin's eyes widened. 'What about the others? For day seven and fourteen. Why aren't you giving me the whole lot?'

'We simply don't carry enough stock to give you all the doses,' I said. 'Your GP will be able to order the rest, though, don't worry.'

'Don't worry? How can I not worry when I might have rabies and you're not treating me properly?'

He was in a real state and it seemed as if whatever I said wasn't going to make any difference.

'This is the regimen, Kevin, and this is enough medicine to get you through until your GP orders some more. Nobody is going to put you at risk, I can assure you of that.'

It was no good; panic had taken hold. He jumped off the bed and started pacing the room, his rapid breath now bordering on hyperventilation.

'I want to know that I have enough medicine. You can't just send me away without treating me,' he said.

I called over to Mandy to bring Kevin some water and then tried to get him to sit down again.

'We only keep a small stock of the vaccine to tide people over for the first couple of doses,' I said. 'And I can't clear out the fridge of it completely in case somebody else needs it.'

It took some time for Mandy and me to calm him down, but even after that he insisted he wasn't leaving until he had enough vaccine to see him through the entire process. The doctor half of me felt desperately sorry for him for having to go through something that was clearly traumatic, but the worn-out working mother was getting impatient that he was unable to listen to what I was saying. So eventually, I had to lay it on the line for him.

'Look, Kevin, I simply can't give you any more vaccine. Make an appointment with your GP tomorrow and they will order the last two doses. You have enough to ensure that you're in no danger. I can't do any more than that, I'm sorry.'

He finally and grudgingly accepted that he wasn't going to get anywhere however long he sat there, and he agreed to go home, taking the vaccine he'd been offered.

Kevin was clearly an educated young man, but the stress of the situation had got the better of him. He'd had the correct treatment to prevent him from developing the disease but, between getting bitten and arriving at Heathrow, he'd somehow decided he definitely had rabies. I'd almost lost patience with him that afternoon, but lying in bed later that night, thinking about his plight, I reminded myself of his age and circumstances: abandoning the project he was working on, leaving his friends and travelling back all on his own, not to mention worrying that he might have rabies. No doubt his fear was stoked by the popular image of feral dogs foaming at the mouth . . .

It was with relief that I realized my eyes now felt very heavy in the way that they do when sleep is about to envelop you and carry you away. Hoping for at least a few hours of peace and tranquillity, I closed them, but at that very second the drilling started; so loud that it might have been coming from the little ensuite bathroom a few feet away. Jesus Christ! I'd moved over to Terminal 5 to escape the builders in Terminal 4, but it looked like there was a fat chance of that. I'd even got used to sleeping through it – well, semi-sleeping – that was what my earplugs were for. Tonight, though, I just wanted it to stop. Tonight, I needed real sleep.

I couldn't say what time I eventually dropped off but it was short-lived. At 4.30am a call came in to tell me there was sickness aboard a flight coming in from Los Angeles, and a lot of it – perhaps a dozen people. My heart sank. D&V – that's diarrhoea and vomiting to the uninitiated – was something I dealt with all the time, and although not pleasant it was quite commonplace, particularly with children. What was much more out of the ordinary was a dozen people going down with it on the same flight, including a couple of the crew.

'OK, can you tell me what stand the plane is going to be on?' I said wearily, knowing that it would be at least a couple of hours before the flight landed.

After that it was hopeless, though. Exhausted or not, my brain habitually clicked into gear the second I hung up the phone. What's the sickness going to be this time? Is it going to be something routine or am I going to have to hold an entire planeload of pissed-off people hostage again while I rule out something sinister? Tonight this was especially true because there was more than one sick passenger involved so it would take a while, making me just the annoying, slightly exhausted-looking individual in a white coat, getting in everyone's way and preventing them continuing their onward journey.

I also had it in mind that the swine flu epidemic was in its early stages, so although the flight was from LA rather than Central America it would be important to exclude this as a cause of everyone's symptoms.

Eventually, I dragged myself out of bed, calling out to the HCOs who were in the office just outside the bedroom. Sarah appeared first. As always her dark hair looked immaculate, as if she hadn't spent the night sleeping in a chair. I sometimes wondered how she did it. I got to sleep in a bed and never looked as good and well rested as she did. Sarah was lovely, warm and friendly with twin daughters – she took a maternal interest in my two little ones and always wanted to see pictures of them.

'Twelve people on a flight from Los Angeles, Sarah, all very sick,' I said. 'We need to meet the plane and check everyone thoroughly. We've got a while yet before it lands but we'll need to be on standby.'

'What a lovely way to start the morning,' she said. 'I'll go and get Sinead.'

Sinead had that loud, authoritative tone that you ignored at your peril, and in cases like this, when there were a lot of sick people to deal with, she was a real asset; the jewel in the crown as far as HCOs went.

The thought of so many sick people and my lack of shut-eye meant that my stress levels were simmering that morning. Quite a few of the afflicted apparently had high temperatures, and that was a symptom that could never be taken lightly. I was going to have to battle to get into a paper suit whether I liked it or not. One thing was clear: with that many cases of sickness on one flight, I was going to have to examine every person affected, taking details of all their symptoms as well as their medical history, all while they were still in the throes of excreting whatever they happened to be excreting within an aircraft's limited toilet space.

As usual at the door of a plane, Sinead, Sarah and I were met by a bevy of immaculate cabin crew who, despite having flown through the night, were as bright and breezy as hell, looking top-to-toe perfect: hats, hair, tailored jacket, the lot! The contrast between how pristine they looked and how plain and worn-out I felt never failed to jar. And then it was on to the plane to get the job done with all eyes on me. The purser greeted me as I stepped aboard, telling me that she had suffered slightly with sickness herself but was holding it together. Many of the other affected passengers, plus a couple of crew members, weren't faring so well.

'There didn't seem to be any sickness when we took off, Doctor,' the purser said. 'Everyone who boarded the flight in Los Angeles seemed happy and healthy. No problems at all. It all started after we'd served all the meals. Do you think it might be food poisoning?'

'Any coughing and sore throats?' I said.

The purser shook her head. 'None that I know of. A few people with high fevers, though.'

This was good news as far as swine flu was concerned, and I suspected the purser could well be right about the food poisoning.

A tall man in a suit made his way towards me from the front of the plane. He didn't look sick, but he didn't look happy either.

'Doctor, can I have a word?' he said.

'If you're quick,' I said. 'Are you ill, sir?'

'No I'm not,' he said. 'But whatever this on-board sickness is, I think you could at least let the first-class passengers off the plane, don't you?'

I opened my mouth to reply but Sinead got in first.

'Oh, breathing different air up there are we, sir?' she said.

This was what I meant when I said she was an asset. No stroppy passenger could out-strop Sinead, first class or otherwise. The man flushed and turned away, slinking quietly back to his seat. I didn't have to say a word.

'OK, let's get this show on the road,' Sinead said.

It wasn't difficult to spot the afflicted as I made my way along the aisle. They were the grey ones; a smattering of them clutching white paper bags in front of their faces, shoulders up around their ears.

'I think the crew are probably right – this is going to turn out to be food-related,' I told Sarah. 'Still, we're going to have to check on everyone who's been affected. I think it's best if I see them one at a time in a galley area at the rear of the plane.'

'No problem,' Sarah said, but her face told a different story.

The HCOs and nearby crew sprang into action, while I headed down the plane to set up my ad-hoc medical station, which, as it turned out, was no picnic. Running a clinic in the tiny galley of a packed aircraft was hazardous enough, without the addition of compromised passengers hurtling back and forth to the toilet without a second to spare. There I was with my stethoscope, my thermometer and a pen and piece of paper to get people's names, trying to get a bit of wriggle room while the crew were busy tidying up around me. Just imagine trying to do your job in a space you can barely turn around in. One of the passengers, a large lady who really was quite weak and poorly, was having to perch precariously on one of the little jump seats in the galley while I was examining her. I had to get one of the stewards to keep her on the seat and hope to God that she didn't throw up all over him. And with the air conditioning now switched off, it was boiling. I could feel my hands were sweating under my gloves, and the smell of vomit mingled with the planeload of hot, sweaty passengers was pretty disgusting.

I'd only had to examine a couple of them to reach a diagnosis. As I'd suspected, the familiar call of 'chicken or fish' along the aisle that day was more culinary Russian roulette than it was a meal preference. These passengers had food poisoning – and quite nasty at that. When something like this happens, Environmental Health have to be informed right away. Luckily, the crew had been savvy enough to save some of the suspect chicken, unopened, so it could be sent off to be tested.

I made my way slowly through the queue of patients, some

sicker than others, while a mix-tape of retching and unpleasant noises — you can just imagine — rang in my ears. Sinead and Sarah, meanwhile, took an inventory, checking on the general wellbeing of the other passengers and passing out information on what they needed to do if they got sick later. It was bad enough that there were so many passengers down, but, as usual, everyone who wasn't stricken was just desperate to get off the flight, having boarded it some eleven hours ago in Los Angeles. Subsequently, it felt like I was in a race against time before all the healthy 'shut-ins' revolted and stormed the doors. Mercifully, they did not and, finally, an hour and a half later, our work there was done.

I was beyond exhausted when I got home at 11am. It was one of those rare times when I asked myself, should I still be doing this? Was this really the best job for a mum with two young boys? Crashing through the front door, I was greeted by a beaming husband, fresh and ready to start his day, along with two excitable boys who'd missed their mummy. I headed into the kitchen and flopped down at the table, turning on the coffee machine, while Chris grabbed his coat and planted a happy kiss on my lips. There was no concealing his eagerness to liberate himself from the shackles of our beautiful but demanding boys; in fact if his feet had been wheels I'd surely have smelled burning rubber as he sped around the house, gathering his belongings.

'Darling, is there *any* way you could hang back this morning, just for a little while?' I said.

I knew it wasn't going to go down well, but by the look on his face you'd think I'd just asked him for a kidney.

'Hang back?' He was clearly appalled at the very thought.

'Just for an hour so I can have a sleep. I actually haven't slept at all,' I said. 'Not a wink.'

Chris sighed and closed his eyes. 'You were out all day yesterday and all night working, Steph, and now I have to get to work. You know I do.'

'I know but . . .'

'I'm knackered too,' he said. 'Wilf kept me up half the night as usual.'

Our second son Wilf was a notoriously terrible sleeper, in fact he didn't sleep through the night once in two years, so I felt Chris's pain. If only I'd been able to crash out on the couch while Henry and Wilf ran amok around me it wouldn't have been so bad, but like all children of the small variety they needed attention. In fact, at some point, soon after Chris had left for work, I was going to have to get my act together and get them out of the house – exhausted or not. I'd probably take them over to see Jane who lived just half an hour's drive away and – as she usually worked three twelve-hour shifts each week – also had the day off. Jane was always so great with my kids and an amazing support for me. The epitome of calm,

Jane would help entertain the boys when I was feeling frazzled while simultaneously managing to keep me buoyant. It was at times like this, when I hadn't slept for almost twenty-four hours, that the struggle to get through the day with a toddler and baby was real, and Jane was as much a godsend as she was a great friend.

As Chris banged the front door shut I closed my eyes and took a deep breath. I thought about June, who'd just the day before asked me if I was finding it terribly difficult, juggling motherhood with my job, especially with a young baby and a toddler. When Henry was born, I'd fretted that nobody else could look after him quite as well as I could, but my desire to work and use my brain (and not waste my education and two degrees) meant that there was never any question of me quitting to become a full-time mum, and now it just seemed natural for Chris and me to both be working parents – we loved our children but we loved our work too. I thought about it for a while as I sat there listening to Wilf relentlessly banging his cup on the kitchen table and Henry demanding that I admire his latest Lego creation. I might have been dog-tired that day and on many days to follow, but I certainly wasn't ready to give up. Not just yet.

# 16

# seasons come

REMEMBER THE VOLCANIC ASH CLOUD? Those eruptions that happened at the unpronounceable Eyjafjallajökull in Iceland, and caused unprecedented disruption to air travel across Europe in April 2010? That was another stand-out few days. For a week, ash from the eruption covered huge areas of Northern Europe, paralysing airlines in about twenty countries and causing them to shut down their airspace, which affected around ten million travellers – the highest level of air travel disruption since the Second World War. It was actually a relatively small event as far as volcanic eruptions went, but because the volcano's ash had spread unusually far and stayed for longer than usual in the atmosphere, the resulting ash plume caused chaos in the air for nearly a month.

Over this period global airlines cancelled around 95,000

flights and lost about £1.1 billion in revenue. There was no choice: the fine, abrasive particles clog fuel and cooling systems, and erode metal. British airspace closed for six days, and they were very strange days at Heathrow. When the ash cloud really kicked in, I called Dr Thana to get the lowdown.

'Is the unit even open?' I asked. 'I mean, there are no flights. Am I coming in tomorrow?'

'You need to come in even if it's just to field the regular calls,' he said. 'At least it'll be a quiet shift.'

That was an understatement; it was a complete doss. When I got to Heathrow, all the aircraft were grounded and the airport was like a ghost town. It was beautiful weather, and as I looked up at the clear, blue sky it seemed unfamiliar without the usual criss-crossed white lines. An airport without passengers is pointless, not to mention eerie, and all I did was read books and watch TV. I also went to bed at a normal time and, in contrast to home, got a full night's sleep. It felt as though I was on a really dull holiday, which, for me, was bliss.

Once the fog cleared, so to speak, I expected chaos, with the floodgates opening and thousands of delayed travellers pouring in and out of the airport, but that wasn't the case in Arrivals. Departures was probably bedlam with thousands of desperate passengers trying to get away, but although the incoming flights were a little busier, we were relatively unaffected as things got back to normal. It may have been an anti-climax as far as work was concerned, but it was an extreme example of just how vulnerable air travel is to whatever nature can throw at it.

Most of the time the normal vagaries of the weather affected Departures more than it did Arrivals, so most natural occurrences, like a lot of snow or maybe fog, would render Departures chaotic, creating a sort of refugee camp air about the place: travellers arriving but not able to leave. If weather conditions meant that flights were diverted from landing at Heathrow, then we at HCU simply had some respite from the flow of work. In fact we relished a mild natural disaster or crazy weather, for this reason. Even if someone fell ill in Departures there wasn't anything for us to do, they just called the paramedics, no matter what was wrong with them. In truth, nobody was very concerned about what infectious diseases were leaving the country; that was someone else's problem. We were all about what might be coming in, and besides that, the legal framework under which we at Port Health worked did not cover Departures.

There were other seasonal variations that affected us at Port Health. The great September student rush, for example, but that wasn't just a one-off; it happened every year and was nothing short of a nightmare. Throughout much of my career at Heathrow, September and the beginning of October was the time when thousands upon thousands of foreign students arrived in the UK, ready for the start of their college and university terms, and it was generally chaotic. The students came from all over the world, some from South and Central America, and many from India and Pakistan, but the largest number came from China. All these were countries with high rates of TB, so anyone coming from such a country had to either be X-rayed or have the X-rays they had brought with them checked. During this time we would do hundreds of X-rays a day in our unit, and airport staff would put rows of extra seats in the immigration hall to accommodate the influx. The queue would spill out of HCU and wind up and down the immigration hall, and everyone who worked in the unit hated it. There was no opportunity for breaks and, starting as soon as the first flights came in, we often didn't finish till two or three in the morning.

Part of the hell of these days was keeping order among many of the students, even before they'd been X-rayed. Queuing is something we Brits are good at. We're generally polite – overly so – and it's ingrained in us. Most of us are massively indignant when we're lining up for something and someone pushes in, but more often than not we just tut loudly or roll our eyes. Some other nationalities had no such qualms about ignoring queues, or perhaps they just didn't get the concept. Many of them would wander into HCU, striding straight past a line of a couple of hundred people and making their way straight up to the desk. Consequently, I'd spend 50 per cent of my day shouting, 'Get to the back of the queue,' to confused students waving papers at me. Chinese students would often have booklets issued by their government, stating which vaccinations they'd had and the results of their chest X-rays, etc., so aside from my usual duties I'd be checking documents and writing down the names and numbers of students, so this was ready to input into the computer system later. It was basically all hands on deck because the sheer numbers were so extraordinary.

This was also one of those systems that was open to abuse, and very difficult to police. Back then, foreign students were encouraged because they bring so much money into the country – fees for foreign students are high in comparison to those of students living in the UK and the EU – so generally, as long as someone can afford to pay the fees and has secured a place at a school, college or university, they are eligible for a student visa. Consequently, among the thousands of legitimate students who made up the vast majority of those I dealt with each autumn, there was a small but significant number of people who were simply using the student visa system as a way of coming to live in the UK.

We saw some students arriving who had enrolled in so-called 'language schools', which seemed questionable! Most language schools are of course completely respectable but there was an address of one particular institution that came up quite frequently, and that we all thought was suspect. In the end, one of the HCOs went along and checked it out one day, reporting back that it was in fact a flat above a busy high street in central London. Despite having a very grandiose name, it just seemed bogus; a way of coming into the country on a valid student visa. Whether the 'school' offered any teaching, I don't know, but the HCO said it didn't look big enough to cope with the numbers purporting to be coming to study there. Certainly some 'students' never intended to actually study, and would end up disappearing into the ether with a job and a life somewhere in the UK. The issue of bogus students became a scandal in the media in the mid-noughties and the process was gradually tightened up. The government improved checks on those applying for student visas and on the institutions sponsoring them.

It wasn't just the dodgy language schools that were the problem, either. Immigration would often interview people coming through who were coming to the UK to do an MBA (Master of Business Administration) who didn't speak a word of English. Of course, all the business courses in the UK are taught in English, so how the hell was that going to work? There was no way you could enrol in a high-level course if you didn't speak the language, because universities and colleges expect international students to pass certain tests to ensure they can understand and write the language to a sufficient standard to partake fully in their courses.

By the time I left Heathrow, student numbers had dropped and September was far quieter.

The flood of incoming students exacerbated an all-year-round problem: the risk of malaria coming into the UK. Many students came from countries where that might be an issue. Where flights landed from such countries, including South East Asia and large parts of Africa, cabin crew were required to spray the whole cabin with mosquito spray before disembarkation. Malaria is caused by a parasite transmitted by mosquito bites, and so the idea was to prevent any mosquitoes that might have somehow got on board the plane at the country of origin from disembarking with the passengers. Later, in 2016, the Department of Transport expanded the number of countries whose flights were to be sprayed to include those confirmed to have the Zika virus, to prevent the spread of this too.

Once the spraying was done, a member of the crew would drop the empty canisters off with us, and the HCOs were required to log them. We hadn't the faintest idea why we were expected to complete this task, as none of the information went anywhere – it seemed to stop dead with us. It was just one of those things HCU did: logging empty mosquito spray canisters. During the mayhem of the en masse student arrival, someone from a Chinese air crew would invariably come into

HCU, smiling and waving a canister at us, informing us that their plane had been sprayed for mosquitoes. On one occasion a petite girl from Air China was unfortunate enough to be delivering her canister for logging while Sinead was on duty.

'So you're saying that massive jumbo jet full of people that we've just had come through here has been completely decontaminated with one can of Deet?' she said.

The girl looked blankly at Sinead, not knowing what on earth she was talking about, but Sinead continued undaunted.

'I mean, how have you managed to cover the whole aeroplane, including the upper deck, with one can of spray? How is that even possible?'

To be honest, I'm not sure she'd have understood Sinead's robust Irish brogue even if she'd spoken the language fluently. In the end she just placed the canister gently on the desk and backed out, smiling but without saying a word.

# 17

# the pact

My phone pinged a message from Chris and I knew it was 6pm. It was my nightly picture of the boys at bath time. Chris knew that most evenings I'd be too busy to take a phone call, and the boys were too little to talk to anyway, so a nightly snap of them both getting ready for or having their bath was perfect and always lifted me, whatever I had going on at work. I was just staring down at the snap of my beautiful boys, when the office phone rang.

'Jack here, Doctor. We've got a young girl we need some help with. She's come in on a Delta flight from the US.'

'OK, Jack, what's the problem with her?' I asked, slipping my phone in my pocket.

'She's behaving really strangely,' Jack said. 'She's got no return ticket and when we ask her anything about anything, she's extremely cagey, distressed even. She says she's going to Germany on holiday but she doesn't know anyone or even where she's staying once she gets there.'

Immigration had pulled the young woman to one side and taken her into one of the rooms there, but when they questioned her further she completely clammed up. That's when Jack had called me.

'Could you come and check her over please, Dr Green? She really doesn't look too well.'

I headed to the room where the young woman was being held and chatted briefly with the IO there who brought me up to speed on what had happened, filling in the gaps with the scant information she'd garnered from her. When I walked into the room and saw the girl sitting there, I was struck by just how desolate she looked. She was upright on an examination bed, fists clenched on her knees, but didn't even look up at me as I crossed the room and placed my bag down on the nearby table.

I spoke softly. 'Hello there, I'm Dr Green. What's your name?'

'Nat,' she said, still not looking up.

'What is that short for?' I asked.

She shrugged, raising her gaze to mine, just for a split second. 'Natalia, but I don't care for that.'

'OK, Nat it is then.'

Pools of dark skin under her eyes told me that the girl hadn't slept for days. She wore no make-up and despite her dark colouring was deathly pale. Her fingernails were bitten to the cuticle and her thick black hair fell lankly on either side of her face. She was in her mid-twenties, I thought probably of Hispanic origin, slight but not emaciated, and generally quite unremarkable, except for the fact that instead of looking petrified like most people who had been detained by Immigration she looked flat, blank and resigned. I pulled a chair closer to the bed and sat down.

'Is it OK if we just have a quick chat?' I said.

'Why am I here?' Her voice was a monotone.

Understandable, I suppose; she'd been questioned by Immigration, not been allowed through and then put into a room on her own. That's enough to unsettle anyone travelling to a foreign country on their own, let alone a young woman with possible mental health problems.

This certainly wasn't going to be a straightforward assessment.

'Some of the Immigration Officers were a little bit worried about your welfare,' I said.

'Were they?' she said. 'If they were that worried, why did they put me in here?'

'Well, you didn't want to say why you were here and how long you were staying,' I said. 'Also, you don't have a return ticket to the States and you don't seem to know anyone in Europe, which is always going to arouse suspicion with Immigration.'

Nat shook her head. 'I didn't really like those guys.'

'I know, but they're just doing their job,' I said. 'Just like it's my job to ask you if there's anything you might want to talk about.'

'What do you mean?' Nat hunched over, as though she were protecting herself.

'Well, I'm not an Immigration Officer, I'm a doctor,' I said. 'I'm not here to investigate you or anything like that; I'm just here to find out if you're OK, and if you're not OK then I'm here to help you.'

'Help me how?' she said. 'What makes you think I need help? What makes you think I'm not OK?'

'You honestly don't look very well to me, Nat,' I said. 'You seem very down and I'm worried about you, and I expect there are people back home who are worried about you as well.'

'I'm not so sure about that,' she said.

'OK, well, whatever is going on, I don't want you to be suffering through it on your own. I want to get you any help you might need, and at this moment I don't think sitting in a room at Heathrow Airport is the best place for you to be.'

She put her hands over her mouth, like she was about to pray, then she muttered. 'I know where I need to be; they just wouldn't let me go there.'

'Well, maybe if you talk to me and tell me, I might be able to help you,' I said.

Finally, she looked up at me again. 'I'm really thirsty.'

I headed outside and asked June if she'd pop to the drinks machine to get Nat a cup of coffee.

'Of course,' she said. 'Is she OK? She doesn't look great, poor lamb.'

'She's incredibly depressed, June. I can't work out why she's travelling, and to tell you the truth I'm not sure she even knows herself.'

'I'll get her that coffee,' she said.

'Thank you. And make it decaf, just to be on the safe side.'

As June headed off I took a moment outside, trying to work out how on earth I was going to get this young woman to open up. Was she running away from something? Had she suffered some kind of trauma? She reminded me of some of the patients I'd treated on my psychiatry rotation, the ones who had given up hope of getting better. I needed to get to the bottom of what was bothering Nat.

June came back with the coffee and I headed back into the room, where I found Nat gazing at the floor, not even looking up when I came in.

'Here you go,' I said, handing her the cup. 'There's some sugar here too.'

Nat nodded, taking the coffee and then peering over the top

of the paper cup at me as she sipped it. I settled myself back in the chair and smiled at her. Was I imagining it or did her body suddenly seem less rigid; her demeanour more relaxed, just slightly? One corner of her mouth turned upward in a fatigued half-smile. Maybe the simple act of getting her a cup of coffee had helped her warm to me. I decided to plough on with my questions.

'You seem very low to me. Have you felt like this for a long time?'

She shrugged and nodded. 'A while, I guess.'

'And have you felt like this in the past? Has it happened before?' I went on.

'I had depression,' she said.

'And have you had treatment or seen anyone about it?'

'I had some medication for a while, but now I just talk to people online,' she said. 'People with the same . . . you know.'

'Well, that can sometimes be a help, but it might not be enough,' I said. 'You might . . .'

'Nothing is enough!' She stopped me in my tracks so I waited for her to continue for what seemed like ages. 'It's all pointless.'

'What's pointless, Nat?' I said.

She clearly didn't want to answer me so I tried a different tack. 'Do you have a job?'

'I used to work in IT. Lost my job last year. It wasn't all that interesting,' she said.

'So you're a bit of a whizz with computers, then?'

'I spend most of my time on them. All of my time really.'

'On the internet?'

'Mostly, yeah. Like I said, I meet people online.'

'Friends?'

Nat froze, her coffee hovering below her mouth. 'Others like me.'

The look in her eyes were disquieting, but at least I felt as if I might be getting somewhere.

'With similar interests, you mean?' I suggested and she nodded. 'What sort of things? Music, games or . . .?'

She shook her head and quickly downed the rest of the coffee.

It was like pulling teeth, but I managed to drag some more out of her over the next thirty minutes or so: no, she wasn't close to her family and didn't speak to them often; no, she hadn't seen anyone professional; no, she wasn't still taking medication; and yes, she spent all of her time in her room alone and isolated, feeling like her entire existence was pointless. There was a nihilism about her, something I'd often seen in people with severe depression. Nothing mattered: not work, not friends or family, not even life.

'So are you saying to me that your life isn't worth living any more, Nat?' I said.

'Yes,' she said.

'And have you thought about ending your life?'

'Yes.'

An important thing I learnt in psychiatry is that it's OK to ask people about suicide. Asking them about it doesn't mean that they're more likely to do it. In fact, many people experience a sense of relief that this often taboo subject has been mentioned so they can open up to someone who isn't afraid to talk about it.

I sat forward in my chair and Nat looked up at me. 'So hearing that, you can understand why the Immigration Officer and I might be worried about you,' I said. 'You've arrived in the UK en route to Germany with no plans or reason for being in Europe. Can you just tell me why you're here, Nat, because this doesn't seem like it's a holiday?'

Her eyes dropped again. 'I met a boy on this one site.' She said it quickly, as though the words had tumbled out of her mouth without her really intending them to. 'He lives in Germany.'

'So that's who you're going to visit?' I said, catching her blush as if she'd said something she shouldn't have.

'I've arranged to meet him and we . . .'

It's never easy talking to someone who's so deeply depressed, but by now I thought there was at least a small amount of trust and rapport between us, plus I'm fairly certain Nat had, by then, twigged that she wasn't getting out of that room any time soon, or at least not until she'd come clean about her motives for taking such a long trip for no good reason.

'So what kind of website did you meet this boy on?' I asked.

'It was one . . . people talk about suicide,' she said.

'And now you've arranged to meet in person, in Germany?'

'That's right.'

'So what's the plan, Nat?' I said. 'Why are you going to meet him? It seems an awfully big thing to do when you're depressed, to jump on a plane and travel half-way across the world to meet somebody you hardly know.'

'We've made a pact together,' she said. 'To kill ourselves.'

I'd almost known what was coming but it was still shocking to hear those words from such a young woman who should really have had her whole life ahead of her. I tried not to let the shock register on my face, nodding as if she'd just announced her favourite colour. Nat told me she was travelling to a place just outside the German city of Freiburg to meet the boy, who she'd hooked up with on some kind of pro-suicide website. I guess we've all heard about these kinds of websites, and any parent would be horrified to discover that their child has been desperate enough to surf the web looking for them. These days, with the internet and online world touching every aspect of people's lives, suicide and the internet have become increasingly entwined. Studies suggest that suicidal individuals who go online for suicide-related purposes are less likely to seek help and are at a greater risk than those who don't. Nat and a young man she didn't even know had made a pact online to kill themselves together, and to her it had seemed a perfectly reasonable and achievable thing to do.

'I need to get to Germany so I can meet him,' she said. 'There's a time I'm supposed to be there and a place.'

There was no way I could know for sure if what she'd told me was real or just something she'd imagined or made up. My gut told me she was telling the truth, so I certainly couldn't advise Immigration to let her continue her onward journey. Even the remotest chance that she might go through with her plan was too awful to contemplate. It wasn't as if I could even suggest she travel home on the next flight back. She was clearly too sick for that, and who knew what might happen between Heathrow Airport and home?

'Nat, I know you're only feeling like this because you're ill, and I think you need some help,' I said. 'I'd also like to find out as much as we can about this person in Germany because it sounds as if he needs some help too. Can you at least tell me his name?'

'I only know his first name is Karl,' she said. 'That's all.'

'OK, well, the first thing I need to do is get you some treatment sorted out,' I said.

Nat really reminded me of a girl called Diana who'd been admitted to one of the psychiatric wards I worked on during my rotation; she'd ended up becoming my patient, so I got to know her quite well. Diana was suicidal too and in a totally nihilistic way. She was about twenty, fairly bright and I kind of liked her, but the way she described the nothingness of her life was quite striking.

'It's all just shit,' she told me one day when I'd asked if she had any friends or family she could turn to or confide in. 'I don't have any close relationships and I don't want them. There's no point. Everybody screws you over in the end.'

Her existence had literally become pointless as far as she was concerned, and she couldn't think of a single reason to stay alive. It really was the most profound kind of emptiness that I've ever seen, to the point that often when I'd completed a session with her I couldn't think of a reason why she should want to stay alive either.

There didn't even seem to be a massive crisis, as there so often is, but she had no partner and a job that she felt was pointless, mundane and menial. Like Nat, Diana had just slid further and further downward, to the point that no one ever came to visit her. In fact she only had one friend, another girl, who was busy with her life and therefore never there for her.

Diana was one of those patients whose plight really moved me. This girl was dark, and as much as I told myself there was still beauty in the world – beautiful trees, beautiful sunsets and all the rest of it – her misery kind of infected me to the point that I too felt low after one of our sessions.

Diana never had to be sectioned because she was admitted to the psychiatric ward voluntarily, having been found at the top of a multistorey car park about to throw herself off. Mercifully, someone had intervened and called an ambulance and she ended up in A&E. She was treated with cognitive behavioural therapy to challenge her negative thought patterns and with antidepressants, which alter the balance of neuro-transmitters in the brain. Medication has a decent efficacy in those with depression, despite some bad publicity about over-prescribing and concerns about dependancy. Gradually treatment began to bring Diana out of the mire, and I hoped it would with Nat too. Diana had to be kept on the ward for many weeks until eventually I could see some improvement. OK, I wouldn't say she was full of the joys of spring, but she was lifted up enough that I could begin to talk to her about how we could move things along. Nat, I suspected, would need the same care and attention.

Nat didn't even react to my words about treatment, looking neither happy nor deflated that I'd discovered her plan. There was just a flat passivity and no fight left in her. I felt that if I'd said, 'OK then, off you go and kill yourself in Germany,' she'd have been happy with that and gone on her way. She was that depressed.

'I am going to arrange for you to be seen by a psychiatric team who can recommend treatment, OK?'

She nodded and I asked her if she at least had Karl's contact details.

'I don't have a number or an exact address,' she said.

'So how are you going to find him?'

'He lives in a really small village in the Black Forest; just a few houses, away from everything,' Nat said. 'He's kind of isolated.'

'So where will you meet and when will all this happen, Nat?' I was suddenly aware of how softly I was speaking, as if any urgency or the raising of voices might make her clam up again.

'He's given me an approximate location of a cabin. He's going to hang one of those suncatcher things in the window, one that's in the shape of the moon, so I'll know it's the right place. I just go to the cabin and knock on the door,' she said.

I was struck by the poignancy of the story. These two young people, never having met, had formed a secret pact to end their lives together. What was even more tragic was the ceremony of it all: the remote location, the secret sign in the window. I couldn't help thinking about my own children and silently telling myself that there would surely be help for them – both from their family and from our health service – if their lives ever took such a turn.

In Nat's case things were starkly different: she was distant from her family and clearly not a wealthy person and, as most people know, healthcare in the US can be pretty shocking for the have-nots. In the UK, she could be admitted to a psychiatric ward to keep her safe until medication had started to help, followed by maybe a referral to a cognitive behavioural therapist or psychotherapist (waiting lists notwithstanding). In the States that might not happen for those without the funds or insurance. This meant that Nat never had the tools she needed to stop the downhill spiral because they just weren't within her reach. Instead, she'd isolated herself in her room and fallen deeper into despair, trawling the dark reaches of the internet until she found a suicide website and somebody who felt the same as she did. Someone who, like her, wanted to put an end to his young life.

At the end of it all, Nat sat as still as stone on the examination bed, looking up at me with neither gratitude nor condemnation. This young woman was so flat, she was ready to accept whatever fate befell her. She wasn't about to resist any suggestion I made.

Ten minutes later, I called Hillingdon Hospital and arranged for her to go to A&E, where the on-call psychiatry team could assess her. If she refused to be admitted they could detain her under the Mental Health Act (what we know as 'sectioning'), but she was passive and accepting by then, so I was pretty sure she would acquiesce.

After that, I spoke to Immigration who got straight on to

the German Embassy so they might alert the authorities to the young man's situation. There was some urgency because of what Nat had told me; if it was true, he was as much in need of help as she was.

After Nat had left, I called Chris who was often my go-to by way of a debrief. Apart from Jane, there was rarely anyone at work to offer up a bit of TLC. As doctors, we are just expected to get on with it, and I was usually pretty good at doing just that. But having Chris at the end of the phone gave me the chance to off-load.

Nat's was one of the most tragic mental health cases I saw during my time at Heathrow and, as so often happened, I would never know the outcome of her story. There was no ending, happy or sad, as far as I was concerned. Once Nat and people like her had gone out into the world, my part was done.

I do wonder what happened to her, and if they ever found Karl in time.

## 18

# mission accomplished

I WAS STARING AT AN X-RAY when Jane came into my office to say goodnight, tossing a copy of the *Telegraph* down on my desk.

'I'm off in a few minutes,' she said. 'Did you finish the crossword today? I'd like to compare notes when you've got a sec.'

'Definitely, but I need to ask you about a patient with TB first,' I said. 'He came through Terminal 4 and I'd be grateful for your opinion on whether I should try to find a bed for him.'

'Have I seen the X-ray?' she asked.

'No, one of the HCOs did it,' I said.

Jane was always based at Terminal 3, as were the other radiographers. X-rays for passengers in any of the other terminals were performed by the HCOs. Heathrow had a special dispensation that allowed the HCOs to undertake fast-track training at one of the local universities, making Heathrow the only place in the country that I know of where non-radiographers were allowed to take chest X-rays. It seems strange that these days they don't even do X-rays at Heathrow at all. The machines have been removed and screening is done in the community, which did worry me, given some of the things I saw in my time at the airport. What happens if a person doesn't turn up for their X-ray and does in fact have active TB or something worse? At the airport we had a captive audience and could ensure that no one left the airport without being thoroughly checked. Screening in the community depends on a reliable address and a level of compliance from new entrants, which I worried would not always be achievable. But the new system seems to be working and there's no evidence that it's any less effective.

One of the things I liked about Jane was how calm and measured she always was in her decisions. As I was so often on my own when it came to making diagnoses, it could come in useful having her there, helping to make the right call when there was any kind of dilemma involved. On this occasion, I had a patient who had TB. He wasn't coughing and it was borderline active TB, and I couldn't decide what was best to do. If at all possible, we insisted that somebody coming in to the country with TB sought urgent treatment as an outpatient, issuing them with a Port 103 document that stated as much.

If they had a credible UK address, that was always the preferable and accepted course of action. The man whose X-ray I was currently studying was an asylum seeker with no address to go to, so it was going to be difficult if not impossible for me to arrange a follow-up. With the bed shortage at the local hospitals, a decision had to be made on how urgent his need for inpatient hospital treatment might be. This wasn't anything out of the ordinary either. There were very few hospital beds for patients with active TB because it was best if they were cared for in a special side room with a negative pressure system, where the circulating air was kept separate from the rest of the hospital. Otherwise they would simply be recycling the bugs around the hospital to other sick people and then we'd really have a problem.

Jane was always a good sounding board for stuff like this; she tended to favour a straight 'yes' or 'no' approach to decision-making, while I often deliberated. I ran through the case with her and she came straight back with an answer.

'Hospital,' she said. 'He doesn't have an address and I don't think we can afford to send him out into the ether with what might be active TB, raging or not.'

I knew she was right, and there was always the chance that Dr Thana would be able to find him a bed at Northwick Park Hospital, which is where we sent any TB cases and who always did their best to help out if they could. Dr Thana had built up a good relationship with the professor who headed up the respiratory team there, but as usual it was getting late and so difficult to organize anything. Almost all of the TB cases seemed to come in at night; there were never any at ten in the morning when beds were easier to negotiate and you had all day to sort something out. The main reason for this was that Immigration were so busy throughout the day, checking passports, that they often had to interview any waiting asylum seekers much later, when all the flights had landed. It was only after that, that they'd come through to us at HCU and, if they were sick and needed hospital attention, it was invariably difficult to find somewhere to put them.

It took me another couple of hours, but finally I managed to arrange a bed for the man at Northwick Park. I was just hanging up the phone when David wandered in, hands in pockets, looking about as knackered as I felt.

'Dr Green, I've just had a call from Immigration in Terminal 5. They've got someone over there they'd like you to come and look at.'

'At this time?' I said.

David shrugged. 'Apparently the lady's been there a few hours but they've only just got around to talking to her properly.'

Terminal 5 had not long been opened, and it had a lovely, shiny, new health unit with a state-of-the-art X-ray machine, all presided over by a pair of HCOs. It also had an abundance of glorious shops and restaurants where I could spend my hard-earned cash. If it was really quiet, Jane, Mandy, June and I would make a coffee morning of it and all go for a trawl around Terminal 5 together. Unfortunately, the fact that it was specifically a British Airways terminal meant that I wasn't called there much during my time at Heathrow because we never had many patients from BA flights, which tended to have more of a business and holiday clientele. I loved it, though, chiefly because it had a Wagamama.

'David, what's the problem with this woman?' I asked.

'Well, Tom says she's told him she's here to see Prince Charles or something,' David said. 'She doesn't really want to say any more to us, so he thinks she needs a psychiatric evaluation.'

'Prince Charles?'

'Yeah, she's telling Tom she's meant to be here and he's getting in the way so . . .'

'Right. Yes, I think I'll need to have a chat to her,' I said.

Assessing anyone arriving into the country who was thought to have psychiatric problems was another big part of the job. Interestingly, these cases often originated from Japan or America and were more frequent than you might imagine. I assume the reason for this was that statistically most people around the world with mental health problems didn't have the money to travel, but Japan and America were countries where people with psychiatric issues might still have the funds to travel to the UK. These issues were often flagged up to Immigration with the routine question, 'What is the purpose of your visit?' This was clearly one of those occasions.

'Tell Tom I'll be over as quickly as I can, David,' I said. 'Just give me time to get over from Terminal 3.'

'OK, Doctor.'

Getting from Terminal 3 to Terminal 5 was much easier said than done. Driving airside at Heathrow was confusing enough during the day, but at night it could be hellish. Plus Terminal 5 is quite a separate entity to the other terminals; it's further down the runway and away from the Central Terminal Area.

I headed down to my parking space and climbed into my car, plugging the lead of my flashing light into the cigarette lighter socket, before sticking it on the roof. I always loved that. OK, so I wasn't exactly Cagney and Lacey but I did enjoy my little flashing light. If nothing else, it made trying to make my way around the airport a little more fun, which it generally wasn't.

Negotiating the various routes of the airport was so notoriously hard that there was a special training video, and then a multiple-choice test you had to pass before you were even allowed to get behind the wheel of a car and go airside. There were strict rules about where you could park and strict speed limits, but the first and most important rule in the booklet that accompanied this test was, 'ALWAYS give way to aircraft.' As if there was ever going to be a situation where you might think twice about giving way to an A380 airbus weighing about 400 tonnes. I had to learn all the different parts of the apron (this is where the aeroplane sits as passengers get on and off), because if I'd parked in the wrong place I might well have been blasted by an aircraft's engine exhaust.

The problem was that every bit of road looked exactly the same. It was an alien landscape and the map we were all issued with was low on detail and almost impossible to decipher. It's essentially a case of here's a building, here's a road . . . and there's some planes. It foxed anyone new. I remember one poor Spanish doctor on a six-month secondment who was permanently lost the whole time he was here. He regularly called the DO in despair and the conversation would go something like . . .

'I have no idea where I am!'

'Well, what can you see from where you are?'

'Planes!'

On top of all that, when there were diversions (which at night there frequently were, due to maintenance work), the signage was always desperately scanty, leaving you no idea of where the hell you were meant to be going – and that night was no exception.

'OK, Terminal 5 is left here, is that right?' I muttered to nobody in particular. 'Or does that mean straight on?'

It's not as if I wasn't used to swerving round fuel trucks when I needed to, or baggage carts with some poor unfortunate passenger's case flying off, but this was beyond treacherous. There were loads of repairs going on at Heathrow that week – everywhere you looked, somebody was hammering and/or drilling away at something, most often at night when the airport was quiet and I was trying to get some sleep. With several different areas where maintenance was being carried out, there were diversion signs dotted all over the place. I followed them to the best of my ability, turning here and there until I finally thought I was getting somewhere. But as I drove tentatively on into the night, I realised that I was heading away from the terminal buildings. Hang on a minute. What was that over there? Was I . . . on the end of the runway? Oh God, I was. I was literally on the runway. I'd come out of one enormous, terrifying junction, but it was for planes rather than motor vehicles.

Everywhere I turned, there were bright lights, which you might think would have made things easier, but which instead were completely disorientating. I froze. Surely, this couldn't be right, could it? No. I'd made some stupid, terrible mistake and any second now an 747 might be about to land on my car, merging me with the tarmac. 'Promising doctor in freak accident: crushed by incoming evening flight from Cape Town'.

No, the last flight had already landed, I told myself. You'll be fine. Well, that was the theory, but I couldn't be sure. There were still cargo planes and late arrivals, weren't there? They still had to land.

I took a couple of breaths and thought about my options – there were two. As far as continuing my journey went, there was only direction I could go in and there was no way I was about to hurtle down the runway. Instead, I plumped for the second option and called for help from one of Heathrow's night team who are always working around and about the airport.

'I have no idea where I'm going, and I can't see,' I told the man who answered. 'I need a lead vehicle as soon as possible, please.'

As soon as possible turned out not to be all that soon, so I sat there on the edge of the runway for a good twenty minutes, periodically wondering whether I could hear the roar of jet engines in the distance. Eventually, a white van with yellow flashing lights pulled up alongside me, driven by a man who grinned as we both lowered our windows.

'You OK?' he said.

'I need to follow you to Terminal 5 please,' I said. 'I think I've come the wrong way.'

'No problem,' he said, and started his engine.

In the end we did, indeed, drive all the way down the runway. Obviously this guy knew better than I did that there were no more planes coming in, but by now my nerves were in shreds and it was all a bit white-knuckle. In fact, I suspected I might be in rather a worse mental state than any potential psychiatric patient I was about to attend.

I headed to the small, quiet room off the immigration hall. There I met an American lady of Chinese heritage with a kind face, who sat facing me with her hands folded neatly in her lap. Aged about fifty, she was dressed in a smart two-piece suit and pressed, white blouse, which seemed at odds with the black Nike trainers on her feet.

'I'm Dr Green,' I said, sitting down in front of her.

'I'm Mrs Lin.'

'How are you, Mrs Lin? What's brought you to London?'

She looked somewhat surprised at my question, but smiled. 'The man already asked me that and I already told him,' she said.

'Of course, I understand that, but I'd like you to tell me if you wouldn't mind,' I said.

'I'm here to see Prince Charles,' she said. 'At his invitation of course. I have a small gift for him too.' She leant down and took a neatly wrapped package out of the handbag sitting on the floor next to her. 'Gourmet bonbons, specially created to celebrate the Chinese new year.'

'They sound really good,' I said, smiling.

'Yes, he has a sweet tooth, did you know that?'

'I didn't know that.'

'The thing is, Doctor, I really don't want to be late,' Mrs Lin went on. 'He'll be expecting me at a certain time.'

'So he's expecting you tonight?' I asked. 'That's where you're going from the airport? Buckingham Palace?'

'Clarence House,' she corrected, as if I should have known better.

After speaking with Mrs Lin for a few minutes, I had confirmed that these were delusions and suspected she had chronic schizophrenia. She was smart and had a serenity about her that might have you believing every word she said, but that's often the nature of schizophrenia. I knew from my time working in psychiatry that people suffering the condition could be very convincing in their stories, because they truly believed what they were saying while they were saying it. Schizophrenia affects how a person thinks, feels and acts, and people suffering from it have difficulty distinguishing reality from what is in their head. Indeed, the definition of a delusion is a fixed but usually false belief, and it is important to be respectful of such beliefs as they are important to the individual concerned. It's not, as often thought, split personality or multiple personality and most schizophrenics are not a danger to others.

Mrs Lin certainly wasn't in the florid, acute state of psychosis where she'd completely lost touch with reality; people in that phase of schizophrenia are usually so chaotic they'd probably be unable to get their act together enough to book a ticket and board a plane at the right time with the right documents. Instead, Mrs Lin had encapsulated delusional beliefs, which meant she was suffering fixed delusions without seeming particularly unwell in any other way. To look at her, you wouldn't necessarily know there was anything wrong; she wasn't behaving particularly bizarrely. However, you only had to dig under the surface, a little deeper, to see that all her ideas were completely outlandish.

People suffering with schizophrenia or psychosis often link themselves to the hierarchy or authority, such as a royal family or government agency. They might imagine they are being tracked or watched by their nation's security service or have some kind of connection to higher powers. Delusions associated with schizophrenia usually fall into particular categories, a common one being paranoia, where a person might believe they're being pursued by MI5, the KGB or the government of a particular country, or that someone is monitoring them through their computer activity – things of that nature. Another common form of delusion is grandiose, where the beliefs are often connected to wealth, power and importance, and this is the form Mrs Lin's delusions had taken. Chatting to her for a while longer, I found out that she'd been firing off emails to Clarence House for some time in an attempt to make contact. She was convinced that Charles was waiting for her – despite the fact that he was married to Camilla – and that when they met he would finally be able to declare his love for her openly. She fully expected that when she turned up at one of the royal households she'd be given entry and welcomed and, from then on, she and Prince Charles could be together.

I recalled another passenger I'd encountered, this time an American man, whose delusional beliefs were so stead-fast that one might almost accept them as truth. Jonas was a middle-aged man with a pleasant face and bright blue eyes, who wore a leather jacket and a Crocodile Dundee hat. He'd come to seek asylum in the UK to escape the gaze of the CIA, and up to a point sounded reasonably convincing. This was before widespread internet availability, but Jonas told me that the CIA were tapping his phone and mistakenly believed he was a person of interest in some kind of crime against the gov-ernment. None of that is unheard of, of course, but he was also convinced they were monitoring him through his television, which is where the story went off kilter. I'd heard similar tales many times, working in psychiatry, but Jonas's matter-of-fact regaling of the imminent peril he was facing might have been quite disarming to someone who didn't know any better. This was his truth and to him it was all completely real.

What Jonas didn't realize was that although a person can claim political asylum from the USA, it's unlikely to be granted because the US is considered a safe country. If an individual's grounds for claiming are psychiatric in nature, then they can be denied entry to the UK on medical grounds. So a decision had to be made about what to do with him and that's why I'd been called to make an assessment.

Jonas, like many people with schizophrenia, kept notebooks full of scribbling, containing all his thoughts and ideas. He showed me a diary recording all the things that he thought indicated that the CIA were after him, and reiterated that he'd had secret messages, via the TV, telling him that he should head straight to London.

As is often the case, the longer the story went on, the more obviously delusional it became. It's a fascinating fact that people suffering from psychosis sometimes see significance in the tiniest details.

I remember at one point in our meeting, Jonas pointed to the window over my shoulder, which had been left open slightly to let a bit of air in.

'Do you see that window there? Do you see how it's open, just a tiny bit?' he said. 'Well, they've done that. They've done that so they can hear us.'

This is called an idea of reference, where a patient believes that something, however inconsequential, is referring to them. It might be something they heard or read, or it might even be something as innocuous as a pencil on a table, angled slightly towards them. To a person suffering with these types of delusions, events are seldom random, and in their mind the person or people who are watching them will have placed the pencil there. 'They did it.' They see significance in everything where there is none.

There is a certain knack to getting people who show signs of paranoia – and are therefore wary and distrusting – to talk to you, and it was usually a lot easier for me as a doctor to get them to open up than it was for an IO. In a case such as Jonas's, or indeed Mrs Lin's, I'd try to find out as much as I could about their story and psychiatric history (if they would disclose it) before going through a mental state examination. This didn't just mean checking for hallucinations, delusions or abnormal beliefs; it was also important to gauge a patient's mood, be it low and depressed or abnormally elevated. For me, it was important to come across as a friend and an ally, rather than an inquisitor, and if I was able to get that right, it usually paid dividends. There are all sorts of techniques involved. For instance, I would never sit directly facing a patient I suspected of having paranoia or delusional issues, and I'd always ask questions in the third person. For example, instead of asking, 'Are you having hallucinations?' I might start off by saying, 'Some people tell me they sometimes see things that other people perhaps don't see . . .'

It was always this kind of work that I got the most out

of and liked getting to grips with and, because of my background in psychiatry, I was often the doctor asked to attend when something like this came up at any of the airport's terminals.

Once I'd finished my evaluation of Mrs Lin, I excused myself and went to find David or Tom to share my thoughts.

'I'm assuming she's not really here to visit Prince Charles,' Tom said with a grin.

'Of course not, but it's not something she's making up either, Tom,' I said. 'She truly believes her story and needs the right help.'

Tom blushed slightly. 'Right. So she's not well; that's what you're saying?'

'Yes, she needs psychiatric treatment but she's not acutely unwell so it's not appropriate or necessary for it to be given here in the UK.'

Most schizophrenia patients require lifelong monitoring and treatment, even after their symptoms have subsided. Treatment with medications and psychosocial therapy are what's usually required to manage the condition. In severe cases, a patient might need to be hospitalized, but I didn't think that would be the case for Mrs Lin. This was not a situation where the person was required to seek agreed medical attention, in which case I would send them on with a Port 103 document. In Mrs Lin's case I issued a Port 104, which states that the person has been denied entry to the country on medical grounds and details the specific conditions identified.

Still, it's always hard to have to deny someone entry who doesn't really understand that there's anything wrong with them, and Mrs Lin was no exception.

'Prince Charles is going to be very unhappy about this,' she told me. 'I don't understand, Doctor. Am I to be sent straight home?'

'I'm afraid so, Mrs Lin,' I said. 'Hopefully, once you're safely back home you'll be able to get the medical help you need.'

There's no way we could send someone with delusions of that nature off into the night, however harmless they might appear to be. It's for their own safety more than anything. Someone who arrives believing somebody is out to get them, for example, is just going to end up lost and wandering around feeling persecuted in a country they don't know, which might prove even more dangerous. And there was every likelihood that, had she been allowed into the UK, Mrs Lin would have turned up at Clarence House demanding an audience with the Prince of Wales and getting herself into all sorts of trouble. It was never going to end well.

I didn't have the power to make any further arrangements than that, but I encouraged Immigration to make sure she was safe on her return journey, as I always would when sending a person home due to their mental health. Tom promised me that they'd make every effort to ensure that there was somebody at the other end to meet Mrs Lin – perhaps someone from the US Immigration team or a relevant airport official – who could look after her when she arrived and perhaps get her home or to her family. In many of the cases I'd dealt with, patients were quite cagey about their families and didn't want them contacted or involved in any way, so it would be up to somebody in officialdom to do what they could to help them. Of course, if a patient was acutely unwell, they'd probably be taken to a hospital, but that wasn't the case here.

On the plus side, the airline would have to take Mrs Lin back to America for free. They had, essentially, transported somebody who shouldn't have been travelling, so it was now their responsibility to take her back home again.

As I got up and said my goodbyes, Mrs Lin smiled at me as if I were the one who was delusional, but by then I think she'd accepted her fate and agreed to be sent back to America just as soon as it could be arranged with the airline.

Schizophrenia is such a confusing and frightening condition for both the sufferer and the people who love them, but in many cases it can be treated and managed. I hoped Mrs Lin, the smart lady with the kind face, got the help she needed in the end.

## mission accomplished

Now it was really late and, mission accomplished at Terminal 5, I jumped into my car and headed back towards T3 to finish up. No flashing lights or lead vehicle this time, but I think I knew the way, didn't I? That's right . . . straight back along the runway.

# 19

# the last flight

ALL THAT EXCITEMENT I had about working in an airport never left me. Among the many memorable days I spent at Heathrow, one really stayed with me: 24 October 2003, which saw Concorde land for a final time. There was a genuinely melancholic air among the airport staff that day. Concorde and her sound barrier-shattering speed was something anyone over the age of about twenty-five took for granted, and if you were over forty, you grew up with it. She soared above us, back and forth from London or Paris to New York, for over thirty years, but I don't know anyone who didn't stop to look up whenever they saw or indeed heard her overhead. It had certainly featured in my life because when we were kids, our parents would take us to see her at Heathrow. In fact one day as we drove along the perimeter road, we stopped at traffic lights so that Concorde could cross to the maintenance hangars, right in front of us. My brother and I were so excited that we stuck our heads out of the car window, and were thrilled when Concorde's pilot looked down and waved at us.

It was a reasonably quiet time in the afternoon when she was due to come in for her final landing, with a full guard of honour awaiting the arrival, so I headed to the viewing area just before she was due. There were press and media from all over the world and, of course, all the British Airways staff who worked on or with her. These were the people it hit hardest; most of them were in tears as she came into land. It might seem odd that we were moved by the prospect of decommissioning an aeroplane, but it was a strangely emotional moment. I also felt a sense of regret that something as amazing as Concorde was no longer sustainable. Yes, it was old technology but it was also somehow of the future, and to this day she still looks futuristic, unlike almost any other mode of transport or technology created in the late 1960s. I always loved the idea that because of the time difference, you could technically land in New York before you'd taken off. Very cool.

I never got called aboard Concorde, with its high-end business-person and pop star clientele. It's not that they had some exclusive Concorde doctor or anything, it's just that nobody ever seemed to get ill – maybe they weren't ever in the air for long enough – so I never saw its sleek interior.

That day was the end of an era in more ways than one because Concorde was the only plane that never took off or landed late. No matter how delayed the flight schedule was at Heathrow, Concorde's flight time took precedence over every other. While other planes sometimes stacked in the sky, waiting to be cleared for landing, she never did. Her slot was her slot and that was it. There was a mystique and a glamour about Concorde and all the staff at Heathrow were going to miss her.

What did gradually change for me was how I felt about my day-to-day work. Being a doctor at Heathrow was becoming a lot of nothing interspersed with moments of high drama and stress. To use a well-worn TV talent show phrase, it was a roller-coaster journey, which, just like any fast ride, one eventually tires of. Despite all the unique and eye-opening stories I came across, and all the drama that made my work life fascinating, I spent a fair amount of my time checking X-rays, and after eleven years it was getting to feel a bit like Groundhog Day. So towards the end of 2011, with both the boys now in primary school, I found myself looking for a new challenge; something that would still satisfy me intellectually but allow me to use my medical expertise in a different way.

This simmering feeling within me finally came to the surface one morning in 2012 while I was sitting at the kitchen table watching Chris and the boys demolish their respective breakfast cereals – all different.

'I really don't want to go to work today,' I said, without thinking.

They all stopped and looked up at me, three spoons suspended in mid-air, dripping milk.

'Are you ill, Mum?' Wilf said.

'No, darling, I'm not ill. I just don't feel like going in. I will, but I don't want to.'

'Like me with school sometimes,' Wilf giggled.

'A bit like that, yes,' I said.

Chris threw me a puzzled look. 'Why? What's happened?'

'Nothing's happened, I've just been thinking. I'm not really enjoying it any more and I think it might be time for a change.'

Chris nodded. 'I wondered if you were feeling like that,' he said, spooning a mouthful in. 'You haven't been as enthusiastic about the airport lately.'

'You didn't say anything,' I said.

'I was waiting for you to tell me,' he smiled.

'It's just so quiet now and . . . I think I'm bored,' I said, and saying it out loud really confirmed the truth for me.

'So what do you want to do?' Chris said.

Now there was a question. I'd now been at Port Health for eleven years, but things had changed. Jane had left to set up a mobile X-ray unit that travelled around homeless shelters and prisons, to try to cut down the TB in those populations, and with Dr Thana now joining the same team, reporting on those X-rays in bulk a couple of times a week, my two closest allies had gone and it just didn't feel the same. The Health Protection Agency had also brought in a new boss who was based in offices in central London rather than the unit. So the general feeling was that it wasn't the same without Dr Thana at the helm. There had also been talk of stopping the X-rays altogether at Heathrow (which eventually they did), and I thought, God, if they do that the job will be even quieter. Over the next few weeks the seed grew and before I knew it, I'd gone and done the deed. I'd handed in my notice.

My colleagues at work were sad but not surprised.

'I could see it coming,' Sarah told me, peering over her copy of *OK!* magazine. 'You've been here a long time and for a while you just seem to have been going through the motions. The boys are settled at school and you're ready for something new too.'

As for my parents, Chris and the boys, they were all happy for me. Chris knew that once I'd set my mind to something, there was no dissuading me from the path and he supported me 100 per cent.

In my final week at Heathrow, I attended the death of an elderly lady who passed away on a flight coming in from Bahrain, relatively peacefully by all accounts. As I headed down the aisle of the plane to record her death, I tried, as I always do, not to catch the eye of any of the passengers I passed, preferring to smile and give them a fleeting royal wave on the way out of the plane after I'd given the all-clear – all being well. Still, this seemed like a reasonably straightforward case. Yes, the woman was dead, but she was elderly. There was no supposition of an infectious disease and so, with any luck, no real need to hold the passengers up for too long. The purser, a slim guy called Adrian, led me to the woman's body, which was towards the back of the plane. The sight of this poor lady took me aback. She was still upright in her seat with her seat belt fastened. I turned to the purser, who raised an over-pruned eyebrow and shrugged.

'The flight's chock-a-block, Doctor, there was nowhere to put her.'

I looked down at the woman who, apart from the grey pallor of her skin, looked very much as if she'd just nodded off. It flashed through my mind that I'd very much like to look that peaceful and composed when I die, particularly if I'd expired in a public place like she had. The most striking thing about this sad tableau was that the woman's husband was sitting next to her: also strapped in his seat, also very calm and composed and holding her hand. I knelt down beside the man and put my hand on his.

'Are you OK? Is there anything I can do for you?'

286

He shrugged with a sad smile. 'Not for me, no.'

'Is there anyone meeting you?'

'No one,' he said.

It struck me that they'd probably spent many years together, and here he was still looking after her. It was a rather beautiful, touching moment, and a bittersweet way to end my time at Port Health.

At the end of my very last shift there was a small party in my honour in Terminal 3. Most of the HCOs were there, including Mandy, Megan and June as well as a couple of radiographers and one of the new doctors. I wasn't keen at first, telling myself I'd just pop in for a piece of cake. I actually hated the idea of a leaving party with all the fuss and heightened emotion, but like it or not I got one: little cards galore, a big group card signed by everyone, balloons, cake and a beautiful Mont Blanc pen as a leaving gift. I was extremely touched to think my colleagues had made such an effort and were sad to see me go – that meant a lot – but there were no sentimental speeches. Leaving Heathrow didn't really feel sad; it felt right. There hadn't been a moment since I'd decided to leave when I'd worried if I'd made the right decision or not. My time at Heathrow was done and I was off in another direction. OK, so I wouldn't exactly say I was happy to leave, but there was certainly a sense of relief and renewal. That, I definitely felt.

After the party, just as the sun was setting, I got in my

car and started the engine ready for home. It was only then that something came over me – I won't admit to a tear – but let's just call it a fondness, a nostalgia. It had been a fantastic job and I'd had a brilliant time. Working at Heathrow had given me the opportunity to work while bringing up my boys without a nanny or childcare. I'd never wanted to be a working mum who dropped her kids off at nursery at 8am and picked them up at 6pm, five days a week, and because of my job I didn't have to. With a bit of help from my parents, Chris and I had always been able to look after our boys between us, and it had been our respective careers that had afforded us that luxury. So yes, it had been the right job, a fun job, and at times it had been more exciting than I could ever have imagined.

As I drove away for the final time, glancing back at Heathrow Airport in the rear view mirror, I had a fleeting thought about the thousands of people I'd seen over the course of eleven years, coming through the port: sick, scared, difficult, confused, amusing people. Plenty more would be coming through tonight, tomorrow and the next day, but they were no longer my responsibility. I was very much landside from here on in.

# epilogue

SOME TIME BEFORE I left Heathrow, I started doing some work for Marie Stopes International in my spare time, consulting in one of their clinics in Bristol. Marie Stopes is a non-governmental organization that provides contraception, vasectomy and safe abortion services in countries all around the world. The charity lobbies in favour of access to abortion, and provides all sorts of sexual healthcare advice. People who use the clinics in the UK pay for the service and that money is used to fund clinics in less economically developed countries, supplying contraception to enable women to control their fertility. 'Children by Choice not Chance' is their mission statement. I've always supported their work so when I found out they were recruiting doctors to work in their UK clinics, I jumped at the chance. It meant I could drop the boys at school, go and work a 10–2 slot, and still have time to pick them up again after school.

I'd always felt very uncomfortable when families were kept in the zoo-like holding room at Heathrow, particularly those with young children. There were usually detainees knocking about in there for any number of reasons, so I was quite strict with the IOs when it came to sticking a woman and her children in along with them – in fact I was dead against it. When the Conservative/Lib Dem coalition government was in power, Nick Clegg drove through legislation ending the routine detention of children, and these days I am a member of the Independent Family Returns Panel, which was set up as a result of this legislation. Part of the remit of this panel, is to scrutinize all detention of families at UK borders including Heathrow. Before that legislation, IOs were technically allowed to detain families with children overnight, but even then I would always insist they were kept for the minimum length of time, just while the IOs carried out their investigation or for their own safety, and certainly not overnight if a viable alternative could be arranged.

Mercifully, the government has now caught up with that thinking, and the Family Returns Panel is there to ensure the law is adhered to, and that families seeking asylum or being held at our ports are no longer detained for long periods in unsuitable holding rooms. The panel also has a safeguarding role and helps protect the welfare of families who no longer have the right to remain in the UK. Members of these families might be student over-stayers who entered the country legitimately on student visas but have failed to leave after completion of their education; other families might have failed in their attempts to claim asylum.

Because of the shift pattern at HCU, I was able to do a certain amount of this kind of work concurrently with my work at Heathrow, but eventually I began to see a different future for myself. I had long been disenchanted with working on a rota where I'd often have to work over the Christmas holidays, Easter or on a bank holiday. Of course, my schedule was nothing to somebody working in a hospital, five days on the trot, and in the early days I just accepted it. Now, though, after having children I wanted to be with them on special family days and during their school holidays.

These days my work at Marie Stopes and on the panel keep me busy – it's what I love. I find my work at Marie Stopes rewarding because I believe strongly in their mission. Sometimes they struggle to get doctors to work in abortion care because it can be controversial, with certain areas of the press and a fair amount of parliament rather negative about it. While I understand and accept these discussions, I'm very pro choice and feel it is important for these services to be available to women. I don't perform operations myself but I do prescribe the medication for an early medical abortion, which is available for women who are up to nine and half weeks pregnant.

Although there is a common thread of social justice running through these roles, I'm certainly no crusader. But they're all jobs requiring a sense of fairness, and this is what now unites all my work. With the Independent Family Returns Panel, we have a safeguarding role towards the families in the immigration process; and at Marie Stopes International we're providing and campaigning for access to safe, effective contraception and choice the world over.

Despite Dr Crosby's foreboding prediction of a nose-diving career if I stayed at Heathrow for too long, it suited me because – as far as work is concerned – I'm a lone wolf. I work best alone, and if I work in a team I prefer it to be my team. These days I love the autonomy of being self-employed and the idea that I'm not tied down to some prescribed career path. There's probably not another doctor in the country who's taken the unusual route that I have, and despite a few false starts I've managed to discover what suits me and, more importantly, what makes me happy: that I'm at my best when I'm running my own affairs and controlling my own destiny; and that spending time with Chris, Henry and Wilf is, and always will be, the most important thing in my life.

There are plenty of other panels that need the expertise of a doctor or indeed someone who enjoys assimilating large volumes of complex information and making a fair decision. So, moving forward, I see myself continuing in the same vein, having recently been recruited to sit on the Heathrow Third Runway Hardship panel. This was set up by Heathrow Airport Limited at the government's instruction to adjudicate on any claims to do with property and housing that might be affected by the new runway. So it looks like Heathrow is going to be back in my life after all. Well, I did tell you that I'd always loved airports.

# acknowledgements

A huge thank you to the following people:

My family for their love and support throughout the writing of this book and always.

My wonderful friend and agent Lisa Gallagher, for always fighting my corner.

Emma Tait, the most supportive and patient editor a debut writer could have. Thank you for going the extra mile and for the expertise you brought to the book.

Terry Ronald, I couldn't have done it without you.

Sarah Emsley, Fiona Crosby, Grace Paul and everyone at Headline for all their support.

Dr Thana, Jane, Mandy, June and Cindy for allowing me to include their stories.